W9-CCV-651

Must We

Divide History

Into Periods?

EUROPEAN PERSPECTIVES

A Series in Social Thought and Cultural Criticism

EUROPEAN PERSPECTIVES
A Series in Social Thought and Cultural Criticism
Lawrence D. Kritzman, *Editor*

European Perspectives presents outstanding books by leading European thinkers. With both classic and contemporary works, the series aims to shape the major intellectual controversies of our day and to facilitate the tasks of historical understanding.

For a complete list of books in the series see pages 161–64.

Must We

Divide History

Into Periods?

JACQUES LE GOFF

Translated by M. B. DeBevoise

Columbia University Press   New York

Columbia University Press
Publishers Since 1893
New York   Chichester, West Sussex
cup.columbia.edu
Copyright © Éditions du Seuil 2014.
Collection *La Librairie du XXIe siècle*, sous la direction de Maurice Olender
Translation © 2015 Columbia University Press

Library of Congress Cataloging-in-Publication Data
Le Goff, Jacques, 1924–2014
[Faut-il vraiment découper l'histoire en tranches? English]
Must we divide history into periods? / Jacques Le Goff ; translated by M.B. DeBevoise.
    pages cm. — (European perspectives: a series in social thought and cultural criticism)
Includes bibliographical references and index.
ISBN 978-0-231-17300-1 (cloth : alk paper) —ISBN 978-0-231-54040-7 (ebook)
1.. Historiography. 2. History—Periodization. I. DeBevoise, M. B., translator. II. Title.

D13.L44413   2015
907.2—dc23   2015008949

Cover design: Jennifer Heuer
Cover art: Left: *Madonna and Child with Saint John the Baptist and Saint Peter,* (c. 1290);
Attributed to Cimabue © National Gallery of Art (Samuel H. Kress Collection)
Right: *Madonna and Child with a Pomegranate,* (1475/1480), Lorenzo di Credi © National
Gallery of Art (Samuel H. Kress Collection)

References to websites (URLs) were accurate at the time of writing. Neither the author
nor Columbia University Press is responsible for URLs that may have expired or changed
since the manuscript was prepared.

CONTENTS

A NOTE ON THE TRANSLATION

Jacques Le Goff's passing in April 2014 deprived him of the opportunity to review the English translation of his last book prior to publication. With the approval of his estate and the French publisher, a great many small changes have been made to the original text, mainly in the way of correcting minor errors of fact and clarifying points of emphasis and interpretation.

To the author's notes I have added a few of my own, not only to provide fuller citations to the scholarly literature but also to refer the reader to related discussions in Le Goff's earlier work. The bibliography has been revised and augmented as well.

I am grateful to Columbia University Press's referee, Adam Kosto, for his helpful comments on a draft version of the translation.

—M. B. DeBevoise

PREFACE

This essay is neither thesis nor synthesis. It is the culmination of many years of research and reflection about the periods of history, particularly Western history. The Middle Ages in Europe have been my companion since 1950, the year I obtained my teaching license. Fernand Braudel chaired the examination committee, alongside the medievalist Maurice Lombard.

I have carried this work inside me for a long time, then. It has been nourished and sustained by ideas that are dear to my heart and that I have tried to express in various ways in the years since.[1]

History, like its subject, time, appears to be continuous. But it consists of changes as well. Historians have long been accustomed to identifying and defining these changes by dividing the continuous stream of events into segments that initially were called "ages" and then "periods."

I wrote this book in 2013. The pace of globalization, as it is called, has now become so rapid that its effects are felt more directly with every passing day. I have looked back over more than six decades, the period of my career as a historian, but also, taking a longer view, over more than six centuries, in order to reconsider the various ways in which historians before me have thought about periodization, whether in terms of continuity or discontinuity, and the various ways in which they have interpreted historical memory.

Studying these different types of periodization makes it possible, I believe, to detect the existence of what may be called a "long" Middle Ages—and this all the more if we take a fresh look at the various ways in which historians have tried since the nineteenth century to make sense of the Renaissance and what they imagine to be its pivotal position in the history of the past thousand years.

In treating the general problem of how history passes from one period to another, in other words, I examine a particular case: the alleged novelty of the Renaissance in relation to the Middle Ages. The present work seeks to establish the major characteristics of a long Middle Ages in the Christian West that extends from late antiquity (between the third and the seventh century) to the middle of the eighteenth century.

But I do not therefore overlook the fact that the history of the Christian West is part of a global narrative. No one writing history today, or in the future, will be able to avoid the problems that arise in trying to carve up the past, only now on a larger scale. I have written this book in the hope, too, that it may make some preliminary contribution, however modest, to this necessary task.[2]

If the "centrality" of the Renaissance is at the heart of my concerns, together with the obligation to reexamine a widely held conception of the Middle Ages that a lifetime devoted to scholarship has convinced me is too narrow to be useful, I trust I have not lost sight of the broader question with which I began, namely, whether history is a unified, continuous whole or whether it is broken up instead into segments of greater or lesser length. To put the question another way: does history really need to be divided into periods?

ACKNOWLEDGMENTS

This essay owes much to Maurice Olender. Not only has he done a marvelous job as the editor of the excellent collection, the Library of the Twenty-First Century, in which my book appears with Édi tions du Seuil. It is also in his capacity as a historian that I am indebted to him, for he has thrown himself into the task of criticizing, developing, and defending the ideas I put forward here with all the passion, intelligence, and learning for which he is so well known.

I have also been remarkably well served by the talented and dedicated staff at Seuil, particularly Séverine Nikel, coordinator of the human sciences division, as well as her colleagues Cécile Rey, Marie-Caroline Saussier, and Sophie Tarneaud.

I have benefited from the conversation and advice of a number of historians who happen to be very good friends, not only the eminent historiographer François Hartog but also Jean-Claude

Schmitt, Jean-Claude Bonne, and their fellow researchers in the Groupe d'anthropologie historique de l'Occident médiéval (GAHOM) at the École des hautes études en sciences sociales in Paris.

I am greatly indebted, too, to Krzysztof Pomian and Christiane Klapisch-Zuber.

And last, but not least, to my dear and faithful friend Christine Bonnefoy, who after running my office at the EHESS for many years actually came out of retirement to make the publication of this book possible.

My warmest thanks to everyone.

Must We

Divide History

Into Periods?

| Prelude

Periodization and the Past

One of the chief problems facing human beings, from the very first moment of their existence on Earth, has been the problem of mastering time. Calendars make it possible to organize daily life. Almost without exception, they are derived from the natural order of the world around us, using two essential points of reference, the sun and the moon. But because calendars generally reckon the passing of time cyclically, on a monthly or annual basis, they are of little use in thinking about time on longer scales. So long as humanity is unable to predict the future with exactitude, the ability to organize a very long past will not lose its importance.

In this connection a number of terms have long been employed, *ages*, *epochs*, *cycles*, and so on. The most suitable of these, it seems to me, is *periods*.[1] The word itself comes from the Greek *períodos*, meaning a circular path. Between the fourteenth and the eighteenth centuries it acquired the sense of an age, which is to say a historically significant quantity of elapsed time. The twentieth century provided us with a related term, *periodization*.

The concept expressed by this last term has served me as a guiding principle. Periodization is not only a way of acting upon time. The very act itself draws our attention to the fact that there is nothing neutral, or innocent, about cutting time up into smaller parts. In the pages that follow, I shall try to bring out the more or less declared, more or less acknowledged reasons that historians have had for doing this, often accompanied by definitions that reveal the significance they attach to this or that period.

Even if breaking time into segments is something historians cannot help but do, no matter whether history is regarded as the study of the evolution of societies, or as a particular type of knowledge and teaching, or else as the unfolding of time itself, periodization is more than a mere collection of chronological units. It contains also the idea of transition, of one thing turning into another; indeed, when change is sufficiently far-reaching in its effects, a new period represents a repudiation of the entire social order of the one preceding it. It is for this reason that periods have a very special meaning: in their very succession, in both the temporal continuity this succession embodies and the rupture of temporal continuity that it brings about, they constitute an inescapable object of inquiry for the historian.

In examining the relationship between what it is still traditional to call the Middle Ages and the Renaissance, I shall pay particular attention—because these notions were themselves born in the course of history—to the moment when they first appeared and the way in which they were originally understood.

The attempt to make periods and centuries coincide is hardly new. And yet the latter term, used in the familiar sense of a hundred-year period beginning with a year ending in "oo," appeared only in the sixteenth century. Prior to this the Latin word *saeculum* denoted either the world (and the generation of people presently living in it) or a rather brief, ill-defined period bearing the name of a great figure supposed to have given it its characteristic splendor (the "Age of Pericles," the "Age of Caesar," and so on). The modern notion of a century has the disadvantage that a year ending in "oo" seldom marks a decisive break in the history of a society. It is therefore considered admissible to suggest, or actually to claim, that such-and-such a century began before or after the pivotal year and extended beyond a hundred years, or, conversely, ended somewhat sooner. Thus we are accustomed to think of the eighteenth century as having begun in 1715 and the twentieth century in 1914. Despite these imperfections, the century has become an indispensable chronological tool, not only for historians but for all those people, and they are numerous, who need to refer to the past.

Yet periods and centuries do not answer the same need. And if sometimes they do happen to coincide, it is only for reasons of convenience. For example, once the word *Renaissance* came into fashion (in the nineteenth century) as the name for a distinct period, the temptation to align this period with one or more centuries proved irresistible. But when did the Renaissance start? In the fifteenth century or the sixteenth? We shall often have occasion in what follows to appreciate how difficult it is to justify the choice of one date rather than another as the beginning of a period. We shall also see that the way in which this difficulty is resolved is not without consequence.

If periodization is helpful in organizing time, or rather in putting it to use for one purpose or another, it sometimes gives rise to problems in making sense of the past. Periodizing history is a complicated business. Unavoidably, it is fraught with personal bias and shaped by an interest in arriving at a result that will be widely accepted. This, I believe, is part of what makes the historian's work so fascinating.

One last remark before we set off on our way. As Bernard Guenée has rightly pointed out,[2] it was a long while before the field of study we call "history" became a separate discipline, that is, the object of rational (if not, strictly speaking, scientific) study. A body of knowledge bearing on the whole of humanity did not really come into existence until the eighteenth century, when it first began to be taught in universities and schools. Indeed, it would not be an exaggeration to say that the teaching of history marked its birth as a branch of learning. We shall need to keep this in mind if we are to understand the nature of periodization.

1 | Early Periodizations

Long before it had been accepted in historical writing and research, the notion of a period was routinely used for the purpose of organizing the past. This was mainly true in the works of religious authors, who used it to divide time into smaller units in accordance with theological doctrine or with reference to figures of sacred literature. Because my aim is to show how periodization influenced social and intellectual life in Europe, I shall limit myself to mentioning the systems that were adopted there. Other civili zations, the Maya, for example, adopted different systems.

A remarkable volume of essays edited by Patrick Boucheron,[1] inquiring into the roots of the modern phenomenon of globalization, examines the course of events throughout the world in the fifteenth century without, however, seeking to interpret them in terms of a particular historical scheme. Among the many recent attempts to reconsider the long-term historical periodization created and imposed by the West, with the aim of establishing either a single periodization for the world as a whole or a series of periodizations, special notice should be taken of the synchronic comparison of the world's principal civilizations, from 1000 BCE until the present day, with which Philippe Norel concludes his pioneering global economic history.[2]

The Judeo-Christian tradition presents two basic models of periodization, each based on a symbolic number: four, the number of the seasons; and six, the number of the ages of life. Here one observes not only a parallelism but also a reciprocal influence between the individual chronology of the ages of life and the universal chronology of the ages of the world.[3]

The first model of periodization is found in the Old Testament book of Daniel. In a vision the prophet sees four beasts, the incarnation of four successive kingdoms that together constitute the complete time of the world, from its creation until its end. The beasts, kings of these four kingdoms, are destroyed in their turn. The fourth king will have sought to change times and the law, and he blasphemes against the Most High, opposing His designs. But then there will come, with the clouds of heaven, a son of man on whom the Ancient of Days has conferred dominion, glory and kingdom, and all the peoples, nations, and languages will serve him. His dominion, everlasting, will neither pass away nor be destroyed.[4]

As Krzysztof Pomian has pointed out, it was not until the twelfth century that the periodization found in Daniel gained favor among chroniclers and theologians.[5] They then advanced the idea of a *translatio imperii*, according to which the Holy Roman Empire was heir to the last of Daniel's four kingdoms. In the sixteenth century Philipp Melanchthon (1497–1560) divided universal history into four monarchies. A similar periodization, likewise derived from Daniel, was proposed at about the same time in a work by the German historian Johannes Sleidanus (c. 1506–56), *Three Books of the Four Sovereign Empires* (1557), the four empires being Babylon, Persia, Greece, and Rome.

The other Judeo-Christian model of periodization, whose influence was contemporaneous with that of Daniel, is due to Saint Augustine, the great source of medieval Christianity. In the ninth book of *The City of God* (413–27) Augustine distinguishes six periods: the first running from Adam to Noah, the second from Noah to Abraham, the third from Abraham to David, the fourth from David to the Babylonian captivity, the fifth from the Babylonian captivity to the birth of Christ, the sixth from the birth of Christ until the end of time.

Daniel and Augustine both looked to the cycles of nature for inspiration: Daniel's four kingdoms correspond to the four seasons; Augustine's six periods refer, on the one hand, to the six days of creation and, on the other, to the six ages of life: infancy (*infantia*), childhood (*pueritia*), adolescence (*adolescentia*), youth (*juventus*), maturity (*gravitas*), and old age (*senectus*). Both ascribed symbolic significance to their periodizations as well. This is not surprising. In thinking about the distant past we can scarcely suppose that any way of grouping events is somehow neutral, or objective, or unaffected by a very personal experience of time and by what was eventually to be called—the result of a long gestation, lasting centuries—history.[6]

Daniel, telling the Persian king Nebuchadnezzar of the succession of four periods, says that each kingdom represents a time of decline by comparison with the preceding one, until the advent of the kingdom created by God in sending a "son of man"[7] (whom the Fathers of the Church recognized as Jesus) to lead the world and humanity into eternity. This periodization therefore combines the idea of decadence, born of original sin, and faith in everlasting life, which—Daniel does not say this, but he implies as much—will be eternal joy for the elect and eternal sorrow for the damned.

Augustine, for his part, places greater emphasis on a progressive degeneration, by analogy with the course of human life and its culmination in old age. His periodization served to reinforce the chronological pessimism that reigned in many monasteries during the early Middle Ages. The idea of decline gained impetus as Greek and Latin gradually ceased to be taught, and the literature written in them began to be forgotten. Already in the first centuries of the medieval era the expression *mundus senescit* (the world grows old) had become common. Indeed, the theory of the aging of the world worked to prevent the idea of progress from emerging until the eighteenth century.

Yet Augustine's interpretation did not exclude the possibility that life on Earth might yet improve. The sixth age, between the incarnation of Jesus and the Last Judgment, holds out the prospect of redemption with regard to the past and of hope with regard to the future: although man had been corrupted through original

sin in the first age, and then himself corrupted the world in suc-
ceeding ages, he was nonetheless created in God's image. Throughout the Middle Ages, Augustine was seen as heralding a blessed
time of renewal, both of the world and of humanity, which later
was to be called a rebirth, or renaissance.

Efforts to organize time were crucially affected in the sixth century of the Christian era when a Scythian monk, living in Rome,
called Dennis the Small (Dionysius Exiguus) made a fundamental
distinction between what happened before and after the incarnation of Jesus Christ. Later calculations by New Testament scholars
indicated that Dennis was mistaken about the exact date of Jesus's
birth. But whether Jesus was born four or five years earlier than
he had supposed matters little for our purposes. The main thing
is that since the eighth century or so in the West, and now everywhere in the world as the result of a resolution adopted by the
United Nations, all of human history has been divided into two
epochs, one prior to the birth of Christ, the other subsequent to it.
It is true that this amounts to imposing a Western periodization
on other civilizations. But I am convinced that the importance for
humanity of establishing a single standard for measuring historical time outweighs the doubts and misgivings that an edict of this
sort will inevitably arouse.

A number of great medieval thinkers helped to propagate the
Augustinian theory of the six ages of man. Three in particular
stand out: Isidore of Seville (c. 570–636), the celebrated author of
the *Etymologies*, whose *Chronicon* was to exert a lasting influence
on the course of periodization; the English monk and theologian

known as the Venerable Bede (673–735), whose *De temporum ratione* (On the Reckoning of Time) concludes with a universal chronicle of humankind up to 725; and the Dominican friar Vincent de Beauvais (c. 1190–1260), who worked at Royaumont and dedicated to King Louis IX of France a vast encyclopedia in three volumes, the final one of which, *Speculum historiale* (Mirror of History), applied Augustine's periodization.

Other conceptions of time, which is to say other religious periodizations, were current in the Middle Ages as well. I shall mention only one, probably the most important of all considering the renown both of the work in which it was elaborated, the *Legenda aurea* (Golden Legend), and of its author, the Dominican chronicler and cleric Jacobus de Voragine (c. 1230–98). In an earlier book I tried to show that the *Legenda* was not, as has long been supposed, a hagiographic work.[8] It was meant instead to describe and explain successive periods of the time that had been created and given by God to man, the central moment of which was the birth of Christ.

Jacobus defines this human time with reference to two principles, the "sanctoral" and the "pastoral." Whereas the sanctoral rests on the lives of 153 saints (the same number as the fish that were miraculously caught in the New Testament account),[9] the pastoral is bound up with the liturgy and the evolving relationship between God and man to which it testifies. For Jacobus human history is the time God gave to Adam and Eve, which they defiled through original sin. This lapse was partly redeemed by the birth and death of Christ incarnate, and led on, following his crucifixion, to the end of the world and the Last Judgment.

From this there resulted a division of human time into four periods. The first is the time of "deviation," a turning away from the right path that extended from Adam to Moses. The next age, from Moses until the birth of Christ, is the time of "renewal." The Incarnation ushers in a third period, brief but essential, the time of "reconciliation" measured by the fifty days between Easter and Pentecost. The current age is the time of "pilgrimage," during which man's conduct will determine whether, at the Last Judgment, he is to be assigned to heaven or to hell.

More surprising than Jacobus's division of the history of the world into four periods is the one devised by Voltaire in *Le siècle de Louis XIV* (1751): "Every age has produced heroes and politicians; all nations have experienced revolutions, and all histories are nearly alike to those who seek only to furnish their memories with facts, but whosoever thinks, or, what is still more rare, whosoever has taste, will find but four ages in the history of the world. These four happy ages are those in which the arts were carried to perfection, and which, by serving as the era of the greatness of the human mind, are examples for posterity."[10]

Voltaire used the term *siècle* not in the sense of a period of one hundred years, which was relatively new in his time, having appeared at the end of the sixteenth century, though it soon became more widely adopted in the seventeenth. He used it instead to refer to an epoch that represented a kind of apogee, or peak, of human achievement. The first of these four ages for Voltaire is ancient Greece—the time of Phillip, Alexander, Pericles, Demosthenes, Aristotle, Plato, and so on. The second is the age of Caesar and Augustus, illustrated by the great Roman authors who were their contemporaries. The third is "that which followed the taking of Constantinople by Mahomet II"[11] and manifested itself mainly in Italy. The fourth is the age of Louis XIV. Voltaire, noting the advances that had then taken place not only in respect of human reason and philosophy but also "in our arts, our genius, our manners, and even in our government," reckons it to be "perhaps that which approaches the nearest to perfection of all the four."[12]

This periodization, while it admirably illuminates four remarkable ages of human history, nonetheless has the defect, to our way of thinking at least, of leaving other epochs in darkness. And it is exactly this darkness in which the Middle Ages are to be found. Voltaire himself therefore sees them as a dark age—without, however, distinguishing it from the Renaissance or from modern times. His approach nonetheless has the virtue for our purposes of recognizing the importance of the second half of the fifteenth century in Italy.

The influence of the two chief medieval periodizations, the four kingdoms of Daniel and the six ages of Saint Augustine, continued to be felt in varying degrees until the eighteenth century. But the Middle Ages also witnessed the advent of a new way of thinking about time, which began to take shape in the fourteenth century.

2 | The Late Appearance of the Middle Ages

Certainly since the time of Dennis the Small, men and women in the lands of Christendom, or at least those who belonged to clerical and lay elites, believed that humanity had entered a new era with the appearance of Christ and, above all, with the conversion to Christianity of the emperor Constantine in the early fourth century. Yet there existed no official periodization of the past, no recognized chronological break apart from the fact of Jesus's birth. A concern with periodization did not emerge until quite late, in the fourteenth and fifteenth centuries, near the end of the historical era that was the first to be more or less precisely defined: the Middle Ages.

Curiously, even though the concepts of "ancient" and "modern" were already familiar during this period, corresponding roughly to "pagan" and "Christian," the preceding period, antiquity, had not yet been marked off as a separate epoch. The very word *antiquity*, from the Latin *antiquitas*, still signified the condition of aging, of growing old—a sign that the Augustinian conception of humankind, as having finally reached its old age, existed prior to the Christian era.

Beginning in the fourteenth century, and especially in the fifteenth, a small but growing number of poets and writers, Italian for the most part, had the sense that they were working in a new atmosphere and that they were themselves both the cause and the consequence of this change in culture. They therefore thought to identify, in a pejorative way, the period they had been fortunate enough to leave behind. Plainly it had commenced with the end of the Roman Empire, an epoch that they regarded as embodying an ideal of art and culture and that bore the imprint of great authors who were scarcely known to them: Homer, Plato (only Aristotle had been read in the Middle Ages), Cicero, Virgil, Ovid, and so on. But the period they sought to mark off had only one distinguishing feature, that it fell between an imaginary antiquity and an imagined modernity. Accordingly, they spoke of it as a "middle age" (*media aetas*).

The first to employ the expression was the Italian poet Petrarch (1304–74). He was followed in the fifteenth century by other poets, in Florence in particular, but more often by philosophers and moralists. All of them believed they were giving voice to a new morality, a new set of values in which, more preeminently even than God, the apostles, and the saints, man stood out by reason of his peculiar virtues and powers, which is to say in the fullness of the human condition—hence the name they gave themselves, "humanists." It is in the work of a leading humanist of the day, the papal librarian Giovanni Andrea Bussi (1417–75), that one encounters, in 1469, the first use of the expression *Middle Age* where it carries the weight of a chronological periodization. Thus Bussi distinguishes the so-called ancients of the Middle Age (*media tempestas*) from the moderns of his own time.

The expression nevertheless does not seem to have come into common use before the end of the seventeenth century. In France, Italy, and England, in the sixteenth and especially the seventeenth century, it was more usual to speak of the "feudal" world. In England, however, the expression *dark ages* was increasingly employed by scholars to designate this period. And in 1688 the German Lutheran historian Christoph Keller (Cellarius), in the second volume of his *Historia universalis*, was the first to define the Middle Ages as the period extending from Emperor Constantine to the taking of Constantinople by the Turks in 1453.[1] This expression, or in any case very similar ones, ended up triumphing with their approval by philosophers in the eighteenth century, notably among them Leibniz and Rousseau.

It was not until the nineteenth century and the advent of romanticism, however, that the Middle Ages lost their dull, negative aspect and acquired a certain radiance: not only in Victor Hugo's *Notre-Dame de Paris* (1831) but also with the founding in France, ten years earlier, of the École nationale des chartes, and in Germany, between 1819 and 1824, of the Monumenta Germaniae Historica, a society devoted to publishing primary source materials concerning ancient and, to a greater extent, medieval

Germany. Only a few years later, in 1840, Victor Cousin felt justified in observing that the Middle Ages, "having in the first moment of emancipation been accused, blasphemed, and despised, . . . began to be studied with enthusiasm, even passion."[2] Medieval history, having become both scientific and social in its turn, soon displayed an even deeper ambition. With the American historian Charles Homer Haskins (1870–1937) and his thesis of a twelfth-century renaissance,[3] and especially with the work of Marc Bloch (1886–1944) and the Annales School in France, the Middle Ages came to be seen as a creative epoch, a time of luminous splendor (first and foremost, it was the "age of the cathedrals")[4] but also of shadows and darkness. The fact remains, however, that if the term has lost its pejorative sense among historians today, the expression "We are no longer in the Middle Ages" lives on, proof that the unfavorable view of this era has not been entirely abandoned.

Eugenio Garin has studied the unflattering picture of the Middle Ages between the fifteenth century and the end of the eighteenth, clarifying the notions of renewal and rebirth, on the one hand, and, on the other, the somber elements that were used to convert the Middle Ages into a period of obscurity whose outstanding characteristic was ignorance.[5] It was only in the early part of the nineteenth century that adherents of a new, positive image of the period, in particular Costantino Battini (1757–1832) in his *Apologia dei Secoli Barbari* (1824), began to challenge the prevailing view, summed up at the end of the eighteenth century by Saverio Bettinelli (1718–1808).

Dividing history into periods is never—I repeat, never—a neutral or innocent act. The changeable reputation of the Middle Ages over the past two hundred years proves my point. Not only is the image of a historical period liable to vary over time; it always represents a judgment of value with regard to sequences of events that are grouped together in one way rather than another.

Periodization, as the work of human minds, is at once artificial and provisional. In this respect its usefulness is twofold: it allows us to make better sense of the past, in the light of the most recent research, while at the same time reminding us of the imperfections of this instrument of knowledge we call history.

The epithet *Middle Ages* therefore expresses the idea that humanity, having emerged from a surpassingly brilliant period of its history, had to wait a certain time before it could enter another that would be every bit as dazzling. It is usually supposed, as I say, to have gained currency in the fifteenth century, principally in Florence—thus that city's fame as the seat of humanism. The very term *humanism* is seldom, if ever, encountered, before the nineteenth century; only around 1840 did it come to signify the doctrine that places man at the center of society and intellectual inquiry. It seems first to have been used in this sense in Germany, and then in a work published in France by Pierre Joseph Proudhon in 1846. Some thirty years later, in 1877, the expression "humanists of the Renaissance" appeared. The term *Renaissance* itself occurred in counterpoint to the "Middle Ages" only with a considerable delay as well. I shall come back to the distinction between the two, which dates from the lectures Jules Michelet delivered at the Collège de France in 1840, in due course.

If we now look further back in time, we find that historical terminology was neither clearer nor more quickly settled. In the Middle Ages the notion of antiquity was reserved by scholars for Greece and Rome. The idea of a prior era from which the Middle Ages would come forth—an era that had been both a model and a source of nostalgia for the majority of medieval men of learning—nevertheless did not arise before the sixteenth century and even then in a rather uncertain manner. Montaigne, recounting his travels in Italy (1580–81), used the term *antiquity* in the sense that it has for us today, as a period prior to the Middle Ages. But scarcely more than two decades before, Joachim du Bellay, in his *Antiquités de Rome* (1558), had used it only in the plural.

Two points need to be made at this juncture. The first has to do with the importance of Italy in this long history of the periodization of time. During the pagan era, up until the advent of Christianity, Rome supplied the measure of Western time, starting with its mythical foundation by Romulus and Remus in the year 753 before Christ (a way of reckoning that, as I say, did not exist at this time since the triumphant entry of Jesus's birth into Christian periodization dates only from Dennis the Small in the sixth century). Italy owed its prominent place in the medieval mind to other things: its conquest by the Lombards and then by Charlemagne; the presence in Rome of the pope, head of the Christian Church but also of the Papal States; an urban tradition of rule by the "commune," this in a Europe otherwise dominated by monarchy; and the importance of both commerce (particularly with the East) and art. Later we shall look more closely at the specifically Italian context in which the term *Renaissance* was to emerge.

The second point has to do with the transition from antiquity to the Middle Ages. The end of the ancient world was long associated with the conversion of Emperor Constantine to Christianity and its legal establishment (by the Edict of Milan in 313) or else with the return of the Western imperial insignia to the emperor of Byzantium in 476. But many historians pointed out that the passage from this world to the one following was long and gradual, with a great deal of overlap on either side. The belief that a clear dividing line between the two could not be established gained support, and it is generally held today that a slow transformation took place from the third century until the seventh. Following the example of German historians who described this period by the term *Spätantike*, it is now commonly known as "late antiquity."[6]

Another way of conceiving of this episode can be found in the Marxist theory of historical change, where it is associated with a transformation of the forces of production. The most frequently cited example is an article written some fifty years ago by Ernst Werner, a medievalist working in what was then East Germany, who, even if he was not a member of the Communist Party, had nonetheless adopted a Marxian view of history.[7] Werner argued that the passage from antiquity to the Middle Ages proceeded from the exchange of slavery for feudalism. I would be prepared to take this claim seriously if I thought the term *feudalism* had any real usefulness. It has sometimes been put forward as an alternative to the "Middle Ages," the fief having by the eighteenth century come to be regarded by legal authorities as the typical form of medieval landownership. Yet the bare notion of a feudal system fails to capture either the wealth or the dynamic social and cultural character of the period. Surely it would be more convenient if we were to continue to speak of the Middle Ages. And since this name has now been purged more or less completely of its old pejorative sense, I say we should continue using it.

I shall conclude this attempt to demonstrate the existence of a long Middle Ages, and the corresponding inadmissibility of the Renaissance as a specific period, by considering the new perspectives for the study of history opened up by the emphasis in the work of Georges Duby[8] and, above all, Fernand Braudel on the *longue durée*. In the meantime, however, it will be necessary to examine an essential moment in the periodization of history: the transformation of historical writing, originally a narrative genre meant chiefly as a source of moral edification and guidance, into a branch of knowledge, a professional discipline, and, crucially, a subject to be taught in schools and universities.

3 | History, Education, Periodization

By means of periodization the historian gives form to a particu
lar conception of time and creates a continuous and comprehen-
sive image of the past. The result is what we are accustomed to
call "history."

In the Christian countries of Europe two conceptions of historical time emerged that seem at first glance to be wholly incompatible with periodization, yet on closer inspection they turn out to
be no less amenable to it than any other. The first is the idea of
time as a chain. Jean-Claude Schmitt has detected the presence of
a sequence of linked events in the iconography of the celebrated
psalter of Blanche of Castille, queen of France at the beginning of
the thirteenth century.[1] A chain may nonetheless exhibit fragmentation, owing to a break in one or more of its links, in which case
it is not inconsistent with periodization. The second conception,
which Schmitt also examines, is implicit in sacred history. It may

be broken into periods of successive ages as well, as in the earliest part of the Old Testament, where the Pentateuch is succeeded first by properly historical books, such as Kings and Chronicles, and then by books of prophecy.

Indeed, with the exception of cyclical time, which has not given rise to any "objective" theory of history, all such conceptions are able to be rationalized and explained. They therefore furnish a basis, as much in the memory of human societies as in the work of the historian, for the construction of a variety of periodizations.

Western historical writing is generally considered to have its origin in ancient Greek thought, on the one hand, beginning with Herodotus,[2] and, on the other, the Hebraic and Christian thought of the Bible.[3] What is today considered "history" gradually came into existence over the following centuries, first as a particular kind of knowledge and then as a subject to be taught. Without these two developments the need to break up history into periods would not have arisen.

The constitution of history as a branch of learning has been extensively studied. Some of the most insightful analysis is due to Bernard Guenée.[4] In the Middle Ages the works that heralded the emergence of history as a kind of knowledge were of various sorts and their authors of various types. Alongside monks immersed in the history of the Church, or of their convent, one finds court chroniclers such as Jean Froissart (c. 1337–c. 1410) and encyclopedists such as Vincent de Beauvais. A part of their work was recorded on rolls, a writing system that itself reminds us of the continuity of time.

In this world the chronicler came nearest to the modern-day historian in his way of looking at the past. Nevertheless when the first important universities were founded, at the end of the twelfth century and the beginning of the thirteenth in Italy, France, and England, and thereafter throughout Europe until the end of the fifteenth century, history, as the chronicler imagined it, was not the sort of thing that could really be taught. This state of affairs changed only gradually between the sixteenth and the end of the eighteenth century.

Advances in scholarship in the seventeenth century, and the corresponding emphasis placed on locating, collecting, and interpreting primary sources, were of cardinal importance. Two great French scholars did work of lasting consequence during this period: Charles du Fresne, sieur du Cange (1610–88), a Byzantinist and philologist whose writings include a landmark dictionary of medieval Latin, *Glossarium mediae et infamae latinitatis* (1678); and Dom Jean Mabillon (1632–1707), a Benedictine monk who worked chiefly at the Abbey of Saint-Germain-des-Prés, near the medieval walls of Paris, and wrote among other works *De re diplomatica* (1681), the first scientific study of historical documents (diplomas and charters) and, as an aid to their analysis, the scripts in which they were written (paleography). The tradition established by Dom Mabillon in this field was carried on by an eminent Italian scholar, Ludovico Antonio Muratori (1672–1750), who likewise published in Latin, in twenty-eight volumes, the *Rerum italicarum scriptores* (1723–51).

The spread of learning in the seventeenth and eighteenth centuries, particularly with regard to the Middle Ages, produced what

Arnaldo Momigliano called a "revolution" in method: the historian's love of truth was now irrevocably bound up with the production of proofs.[5] Periodization, in its turn, now depended on the method selected for establishing historical truth.

For history to be transformed into a body of knowledge that can be divided into periods, however, it must also be able to be taught. In that case, having a larger field of application, it will no longer be simply a literary genre. The universities that came into being in Europe from the late twelfth century onward did not offer history as a subject of instruction at first, but they did play a major role in making this happen later.

No attempt was made in France, as far as one can tell, to teach history before the seventeenth century. I do not think that François de Dainville succeeded, despite his considerable exertions, in proving that it was actually taught in Jesuit colleges during the sixteenth century.[6] Annie Bruter, however, has persuasively shown that over the course of the seventeenth century the transformation of the educational system, on the one hand, and the nature of historical research, on the other, caused history to be introduced as an element of the curriculum in schools, colleges, and universities.[7] The new place accorded history in the training received by royal heirs also needs to be taken into account. Bishop Bossuet, for example, sent the pope a letter describing the education he himself gave (or arranged to be given) to the Grand Dauphin, eldest son of Louis XIV. Certain publishers and authors managed by more or less clandestine means to obtain information about the content of this instruction, publishing works of their own that both plagiarized and elaborated on Bossuet's principles.

History was taught to other children as well. Schoolteachers modified their lessons to include games, fables, and stories that made learning basic historical facts entertaining. Soon textbooks were available for this purpose, for example, *L'abrégé méthodique de l'histoire de France*, by Claude-Oronce Finé de Brianville (1608–74), a former Jesuit who recounted the successive reigns of the kings of France in the form of anecdotes. *Le jeu des cartes*, by Desmarets de Saint-Sorlin (1595–1676), likewise collected tales of royal personages.

Historical matter now also figured in religious literature. One thinks, for example, of the future Cardinal de Fleury's *Catéchisme historique*, published in 1683. But we mustn't deceive ourselves. History was not yet, strictly speaking, an academic subject.[9] Nor would it become one until the late eighteenth or early nineteenth century. In this regard the French case may stand for many others.

The teaching of history was favored by the increasingly regular publication of documentary materials by specialists who may be considered, if not the first historians in the modern sense, then their closest ancestors. The first were the Bollandists. They took their name from the Belgian Jesuit Jean Bolland (1596–1665), whose five volumes (in Latin) of the lives of the saints, *Acta sanctorum*, represented only the beginning of a vast project that they then joined together to complete. The compilations of original texts, biographical material, and commentaries prepared by the Society of Bollandists developed and applied principles of textual criticism that are now regarded as laying the foundation for modern "scientific" practice. The society's edition still remained unfinished more than two centuries later, in 1882, when the journal *Analecta Bollandiana* was established to bring the work at last to a successful conclusion. Even in the field of religious scholarship, what we think of today as history was slow to take hold until the nineteenth century.

The subject that was taught under this name in French schools during the last half of the eighteenth century—the military preparatory schools created in 1776, for example, as well as the Maison royale de Saint-Louis, a boarding school at Saint-Cyr for daughters of former soldiers—was still devoted mainly to moral instruction. Its point was summed up by the formula *Historia magistra vitae est* (History is life's teacher); its purpose, one is tempted to say in retrospect, was to train good citizens in anticipation of the French Revolution. At least some historians and teachers today would not dispute the justice of either sentiment.

With the creation of the *lycées* under Bonaparte, in 1802, the teaching of history was made obligatory at the secondary level, though its place in the curriculum was limited to begin with. It was not taught in secondary schools in any serious way until the Bourbon Restoration, in 1814, as Marcel Gauchet has shown.[9] A history prize was inaugurated in 1819 as part of the *Concours général*. The following year history was incorporated into the oral examination of the *baccalauréat*, and ten years later, in 1830, an *agrégation* in history and geography was created. I mentioned earlier another important date, the founding of the École nationale des chartes in 1821.

The periodization found in the textbooks of this period agreed for the most part with the one that had been accepted, before the Revolution, in those secondary schools where history was taught: sacred history and mythology, the history of classical antiquity, modern national history. It reflected two concerns of French ruling elites of the era: preserving the place granted to religion, in either its Christian or its pagan form, in official accounts; and promoting an awareness, sanctioned by the Revolution, of the importance of what were now called nation-states.

The nineteenth century was also marked in France by the appointment of trained historians to high political office. Under Louis-Philippe, between 1830 and 1848, François Guizot served as interior minister, then minister of education, and finally foreign minister; Victor Duruy was minister of education under Napoleon III from 1863 to 1869; nearer the end of the century, Ernest Lavisse, Gabriel Monod, and Charles Seignobos each enjoyed an influence that reached beyond the academic world. Lavisse's *Histoire de France*, originally published as a textbook in 1884, went on to become something of a standard national history.[10]

The evolution of higher education in this regard can be seen by considering the creation of chairs for the teaching of history in European universities.[11] History was first recognized as an independent branch of knowledge in Germany. It was there, too, that history was first taught and where it most deeply permeated intellectual life as an embodiment of the national spirit, notwithstanding the country's political divisions. The Reformation gave additional impetus to this movement. History was already being taught in general terms at Wittenberg by the beginning of the sixteenth century and occupied an important place in the curriculum at the Protestant universities of Marburg, founded in 1527, and Tübingen, founded in 1535–36. It also appeared in combination with other disciplines, as part of a chair of history and rhetoric created at the University of Königsberg in 1544; a chair of history and poetics instituted the same year at Greifswald; a chair of history and ethics at Jena in 1548; and chairs of history and poetics at Heidelberg in 1558 and Rostock in 1564. An independent chair of history was finally created at Freiburg in 1568 and later at Vienna in 1738, but the teaching of history seems spontaneously to have spread in German-speaking regions between 1550 and 1650. From the second half of the eighteenth century onward the model for instruction in the subject at the university level was the University of Göttingen.

In Germany there were two great historians who, like Guizot and Michelet in France, did much to make history fashionable, Carsten Niebuhr (1733–1815) and Theodor Mommsen (1817–1903). Sadly, Niebuhr's history of Rome was left unfinished at his death, though Mommsen did manage to complete his own, very famous history in addition to editing several volumes of the *Monumenta Germaniae Historica*.

England also played an early role. Ancient history had a chair dedicated to its teaching at Oxford from 1622, and history in a broader sense at Cambridge from 1627. A century later, chairs of modern history were founded at both Oxford and Cambridge in 1724.

In Switzerland a chair of history was endowed at the University of Basel in 1659.

In Italy a chair of ecclesiastical history was created at the University of Pisa in 1673 and a chair of history and rhetoric ("eloquence") at Pavia in 1771. It was a long while before history succeeded in detaching itself from the older field of instruction with which it had originally been associated, typically moral philosophy if not rhetoric. In the first half of the seventeenth century there was still no chair of history in Turin, Padua, or Bologna. The first chair of modern history was instituted at Turin in 1847.

France, for its part, was slow to catch up with its neighbors. A chair of history and moral philosophy was created at the Collège de France only in 1775 and an independent chair of history only at the beginning of the nineteenth century. At the Sorbonne the first chair of ancient history did not appear until 1808 and the first chair of modern history not before 1812.

In Spain it was not until 1776 that a chair of history was founded, at the University of Oviedo. In Ireland a chair of modern history had been established just a few years earlier at Trinity College, Dublin, in 1762.

The emergence of history as a course of formal study may also be seen, finally, as an aspect of Europe's intellectual preeminence. More or less distant continents and civilizations continued to interpret their own history, and that of the world as a whole, by other, essentially religious means—as Europe itself had long done. As for the United States, it had first to make a history for itself before it could assume a place that was to be very large, in relation both to history and to historical scholarship, in the Western world and, indeed, in the world as a whole.

It was in the nineteenth century, then, that history acquired, at least in the Western world, its distinctive character.[12] Now at last it had become a subject fit to be taught in schools and universities. But in order to be able to teach it, professors of history needed to grasp its turning points. They needed, in other words, a systematic way of dividing it into periods. From the Middle Ages up until then, the most commonly recognized break was the opposition between ancients and moderns, which divided history into two great phases. Little by little a period called "antiquity" took root in the minds of historians in the West, with the result that the notion of modernity became an object of interminable debate.

In the course of this same nineteenth century, the opposition between an enlightened Renaissance and a benighted Middle Ages was reborn. The moment has therefore come to turn our attention to the fundamental issue of this essay: the true nature of the relationship between the Middle Ages and the Renaissance.

4 | Birth of the Renaissance

We have seen that the idea of one period giving way to another as darkness gives way to light was advanced for the first time in the fourteenth century by Petrarch. But darkness could follow light as well. The glorious Greco-Roman period, extinguished in the fourth century, was succeeded in the poet's view by a time of barbarism, the dimming of civilization—hence the need to rediscover the modes of thinking and writing that had been perfected by the ancients. But the "Renaissance," as well as the idea of a splendid era of history that was associated with this name after the Middle Ages, and in opposition to them, dates only from the nineteenth century. They are due to Jules Michelet (1798–1874).

As a young man, and still when the first volume of his *Histoire de France* appeared in 1833, Michelet thought of the Middle Ages as a period of light and creativity, a fruitful and radiant era that drew to a close with the approach of the sixteenth century and the Reformation. Looking back almost forty years later, Michelet noted that in seeking to give a full picture of medieval France, he was the first historian to have consulted a new category of materials: "Until 1830 (even until 1836) none of the remarkable historians of this era had yet felt the need to look for facts outside published books, in primary sources, most of them therefore unpublished, in the manuscripts in our libraries, in the documents of our archives."[1]

But these documents were only a springboard for the imagination, a stimulus to insight. In a famous passage that follows in the preface to the third edition (1869) of his massive history, published in five volumes, Michelet evokes the "voice" of these archives—the voice that the historian hears in the privacy of the places where he works alone. Scholarship is merely the scaffolding that the artist, the historian, must push aside once his labors are finished. Michelet's Middle Ages were therefore the product as much of his personal vision and inspiration as of primary sources.

They also traced out the pattern of his own life and personality. The Middle Ages he once knew—festive, luminous, exuberant— began to change during the course of the 1830s. Following the death of his first wife, in 1839, he came to think of them as a period of gloom, of obscurantism, petrification, and sterility. Whereas once he felt as though he had rediscovered his childhood in the Middle Ages, to the point of imagining them as the womb from which he was issued, now they seemed but a distant memory, not merely foreign but hostile. He longed for a new light. This light was to be the Renaissance.[2]

In a landmark article on Michelet's invention of the Renaissance, Lucien Febvre (1878–1956) pointed out that the attitude of many of the great writers of the first half of the nineteenth century, including Stendhal, Sainte-Beuve, Hugo, and Musset, toward the era between 1400 and 1600 underwent a change as well.[3] But none of these authors, nor indeed anyone else at the time, used a specific term to designate this period. The reason is that historians and men of letters were not in the habit then of dividing history into periods. It was customary to distinguish between "ancient," "medieval," and "modern," but nothing more.

Febvre observes that the term *renaissance*, with a small *r*, was frequently used to speak of the "rebirth" of the arts, for example, or of the humanities. But Michelet, profoundly moved by what he interpreted as a force of resurrection in the course of history, was the first to give the period that began with the fifteenth century in Europe, and above all in Italy, the name *Renaissance*, with a capital *R*. Elected to the Collège de France in 1838, he delivered his inaugural lecture there on 23 April. The prestige of this forum provided Michelet with the opportunity to introduce the new name to an international audience in the years between 1840 and 1860, when it became established as a period.

Michelet was captivated by two figures whom he was soon to write about in his history of France: the duke of Burgundy, Charles the Bold (1433–77), and Charles V of Spain (1500–1558). The world in which Michelet himself lived was an ordinary little world by comparison, the bourgeois world of France in the time of Guizot and Augustin Thierry, consumed by a vulgar appetite for money.

A word of hope, of clarity, of poetry had to come forth if literature and the mental habits of the nation were to be reinvigorated. The word came—and with it, a new age: the Renaissance. But Michelet's Renaissance was not the rebirth or the revival of a splendid epoch that now lived on; it marked the end of "that bizarre and monstrous, prodigiously artificial state"—the Christian Middle Ages.[4] Michelet's pessimism swallowed up an era he had once found reason only to admire.

With his lectures at the Collège de France in the first two months of 1840, the historical landscape was utterly transformed. The Middle Ages had been eclipsed. A star was born, the Renaissance. Michelet could not help but bring it into the world, for, as he confessed, "having met with it in me, it became me."[5]

His opening lecture that semester began with a review of the history of France since Roman Gaul. Arriving at the end of the fifteenth century, Michelet declared, "We have come to the Renaissance through the phrase 'return to life' . . . thus we come into the light."[6] Following on Marco Polo's travels in China, and accompanying Christopher Columbus's discovery of America, the Renaissance seems to him to mark the beginning of globalization. It also represents the triumph of the people over monarchies and nations. He sees "emerge from the Middle Ages the newborn modern world. . . . The central figure was everyone, and the author of this great change is man. . . . Brought forth by God, man is like Him a creator. The modern world was his creation, a new world that the Middle Ages could not contain within its negative polemics."[7]

Whence the title of the second lecture, delivered three days later, on 9 January: "Man's Victory over God."[8]

Michelet conceives of the Renaissance as a "passage to the modern world," signaling a return to paganism, to pleasure, to sensuality, to liberty. Italy had taught it to the other European nations, to France first, in the course of the Italian Wars, and then to Germany and to England. The Renaissance thus set in motion the age of history whose interpreter is the historian. His teaching is dedicated to illuminating the progress of humanity after its long, solitary exile in the Middle Ages.

The lectures of the following year, 1841, took as their theme the "Eternal Renaissance."[9] They bear principally on Italy and on everything that France owed to it. Michelet sees an "interdependence" between the two countries from the time of Julius Caesar, a "fertile marriage," as he calls it, a "long union perpetuated by religion, art, and law." He claims that "the Italian principle that fertilized France is above all the geometrical spirit, the principle of order applied to civil society, the construction of the great channels of communication: Roman roads went in every direction."[10] Thus it was that in inaugurating the Italian wars, the French king Charles VIII "went looking for civilization on the other side of the Alps."[11]

Michelet then goes on to describe a country of superb cities, beginning with Florence, then Pisa, Genoa, Venice, Milan, and finally Rome. Its beauty and its wealth attracted conquerors, who came away with a magnificent haul of treasures, not the least of which was liberty.[12] The greatness of Florence is summed up by the Dominican friar Savonarola, an inspired reformer. Michelet praises the charm of the city and the splendor not only of its cathedral but also of the Basilica di Santa Croce, where Michelangelo was buried. The papacy, he says, is to be admired for placing its power in the service of the arts. Rid of the Borgias, it regained the radiance it had enjoyed under Julius II, the patron of Machiavelli and Michelangelo. Alongside the "dramatic beauty of Lombardy and Florence,"[13] and the wonders of Rome, Naples' glorious history by itself forms the subject of an entire lecture.

Next Michelet recalls some of the treasures that France brought back from Italy; evokes Venice and its "freedom of passion, of physical pleasure, of well being—freedom in the service of art";[14] and then proceeds to contemplate the artistic flowering of Florence, Aldus Manutius (1449–1515), and the development of printing in Venice. Everywhere he notices a passion for engraving. He mentions the study of anatomy and the human body, the magnificent dome of Saint Peter's in Rome, and the influence of women.

Michelet concludes his account of this modern age, this Renaissance, with a mystical appeal to the coincidence of life and scholarship. He emphasizes the historian's obligation to express the unanimous voice of the crowd, for "the modern age is the advent of this crowd, the truly blessed moment when a mute world found its voice."[15] The spirit of hope that infuses the work of the historian leads him back to himself: "I have this hope in me." History, he says, is a resurrection from the dead: "Feeling myself die, I myself am in need of [resurrection]." Apparently referring to the year when he gave his first course of lectures at the Collège de France, he ends with these words: "Loving the dead is my immortality (1838)."[16]

Despite Michelet's lasting influence, the invention of the Renaissance as a period was long credited by educated people in France to the historian Jacob Burckhardt (1818–97). Burckhardt's work *Die Kultur der Renaissance in Italien* (The Civilization of the Renaissance in Italy) was first published in 1860. It was brought out in a second edition in 1869, and then another nine years later in a third edition, altered to the point of mutilation, before a definitive text was finally established in 1922 by the noted German scholar Walter Goetz.[17]

Burckhardt, a German-speaking Swiss who had studied in Berlin under Leopold von Ranke (1795–1886), the founder of the German historical school, taught the history of art at the University of Basel between 1844 and his retirement in 1886. Apart from rather brief trips to Germany and, more frequently, Italy, he spent the whole of his professional career in Switzerland. Initially he had intended to produce a history of the art of the Italian Renaissance, but for some reason or other he abandoned art for civilization (*Kultur*) at an early stage of his preparations. The scope of the project made it both a model and a source for future research in European cultural history generally. I should therefore like to devote the rest of the present chapter to a brief summary of its main points.

Burckhardt's famous work is divided into six parts. In the first part, "The State as a Work of Art," he looks back on the history of the tyrants and great nobles of Italy from the thirteenth century to the sixteenth.[18] He takes particular note of Venice, where he observes that "humanistic culture is, for a city of such importance, most scantily represented," and of Florence, which he calls "the first modern state in the world."[19] He remarks on the early appearance in these two places of "statistical science," among other instruments of power, together with a certain backwardness in the arts, at least at first, by comparison with the other great cities of the Renaissance in Italy.

The foreign policy of the Italian states was shaped by a mutual interest in achieving and maintaining a balance among them through a "purely objective treatment" of international affairs. "With such men," Burckhardt says, speaking of the statesmen of the period, "negotiation was possible; it might be presumed that they would be convinced and their opinion modified when practical reasons were laid before them."[20] He then goes on to consider war as a work of art.[21] Turning to the papacy, which he sees as a danger to Italy, he dwells at some length on unrest in the city of Rome, aggravated by the simony and nepotism practiced by the popes, especially Sixtus IV (1471–84). Forty years later Clement VII (1523–34), a member of the Medici family, which had compromised itself in its dealings with the pontifical authorities, as the Borgia family had done before it, provoked the Holy Roman emperor, Charles V, into sending his troops to Italy, where they sacked Rome in 1527. Yet there is no limit to Burckhardt's praise for Leo X (1513–21), though he too was a Medici. Of this pontiff Burckhardt makes a point of saying: "We shall often meet with him in treating of the noonday of the Renaissance."[22]

The second part of Burckhardt's book is concerned with the development of the individual. A man of this new age, who carries his culture inside him, feels at ease everywhere. Burckhardt quotes an exiled humanist who consoles himself with the thought, "Wherever a learned man fixes his seat there is home."[23] By contrast with the Middle Ages, where the individual was subject to the constraints of religion, social environment, and the force of prevailing custom, the man of the Renaissance could develop his personality without hindrance. This was the age of the universal man—a man such as Leon Battista Alberti (1404–72), architect, mathematician, painter, one of the first great authors of the period to write in the vulgar tongue, Italian, rather than Latin. Burckhardt is interested also in the love of glory, which he sees as characteristic of the societies of the Renaissance. Dante had vigorously criticized the growing passion for personal fame; by Petrarch's time glory was sought not only by individuals and families but also by cities. It was celebrated everywhere, in the tombs of the most distinguished families, in the cult of the great men of antiquity, in the emergence of local celebrities. It triumphed in literature, and writers distributed the laurels.

In the third part Burckhardt examines what he calls the resurrection of humanity, which took the form of a "new birth," that is, a return to a glorious past. "It was not the revival of antiquity alone," he emphasizes, "but its union with the genius of the Italian people, which achieved the conquest of the Western world."[24] Once again, Italy finds itself at the heart of the periodization of history. The ruins of Rome were an object of special reverence. Old

authors were rediscovered and popularized, and humanist literature restored to poetry the eminence it had formerly enjoyed in
ancient Greece and Rome. Humanism developed as much among
the urban professional classes as in the courts of the nobility and
the Roman Curia. Occasional literature and oratory once again
became a familiar part of social life: congratulatory addresses,
speeches of welcome and commemoration, funeral orations, political harangues, academic lectures, sermons in Latin, all of them
adorned with quotations from classical authors. Latin, which had
been on the verge of being replaced in everyday communication
by vernaculars, acquired once more an absolute value in humanist
and curial circles. Burckhardt speaks even of the "general Latiniza-
tion of culture."[25] And yet despite their matchless brilliance, the
humanists failed: their vanity, their artificiality, and (as the rising
leaders of the Counter-Reformation complained) the insincerity
of their Christian faith caused them to fall into disgrace in the sixteenth century.

In the final three parts of his book Burckhardt comes back to
the things that he sees as constituting the heart of the Renaissance. The fourth part looks not only at the discovery of man—the
foundation of humanism—but also at the discovery of the world,
which gave rise to astronomy, botany (and gardens), and zoology
(and collections of exotic animals). In discovering the world, the
Renaissance came to appreciate the beauty of nature. Petrarch may
have been the first to sing of the joys of mountain climbing; the
Flemish School's use of oils gave painted landscapes a new vivid-
ness and appeal. Beauty also made its power felt in portraiture,

both in painting and in literature. In Italy, and above all in Tuscany, biography flourished. But autobiography, associated with the emergence of the individual, began to be written as well. One of the most remarkable self-portraits of any age is due to the celebrated goldsmith Benvenuto Cellini (1500–1571).

The other great characteristic of social life in the Renaissance, which Burckhardt takes up in the fifth part, is the festival. Religious celebrations, in particular processions of various sorts, the feast of Corpus Christi, and mystery plays (performed in front of churches), all preserved their prestige and in some places actually became more numerous. At the same time secular festivals, sponsored by villages or local nobles, took on a quite singular splendor.[26] In the domain of costume the Renaissance signaled both the birth and the intensification of fashion. Purism and preciosity occupied an unprecedented place in conversation. Noble ladies presided over salons; noble men, if they were politicians like the Medicis, over circles. A profile of the perfect man of society began to take shape: his body sculpted by physical exercise, his movements given rhythmical grace by music, he aspired not only to be but also to appear to be.

Women participated in this cultural transformation as equals. Their education differed in no essential way from the one men received. Many women wrote novels and poems; even courtesans were notable for their intelligence and culture. Family life took an artistic turn, with the head of the household conducting a sort of orchestra, and its pleasures came increasingly to be enjoyed in the setting of the villa, the country house of wealthy Italian burghers.

From the painting of the period it is apparent that the countryside was now more closely linked to the city than it had been during the Middle Ages.

The sixth and final part of Burckhardt's work consists, somewhat oddly as it may seem, of a series of reflections on morality and religion that leave the reader with a rather disagreeable impression of the Renaissance as a whole. With regard to morality he detects a universal instinct for evil.[27] Nowhere was a talent for vile behavior cultivated more assiduously than in Italy: "In this country, finally, where individuality of every sort attained its highest development, we find instances of that ideal and absolute wickedness which delights in crimes for their own sake, and not as a means to an end, or at any rate as means to ends for which our psychology has no measure."[28] Yet Italy remains for Burckhardt the scene of "the first mighty surging of a new age" in the history of the world: "Through his gifts and his passions [the Italian of the Renaissance] has become the most characteristic representative of all the heights and all the depths of his time. By the side of profound corruption appeared human personalities of the noblest harmony and an artistic splendour which shed upon the life of man a lustre which neither antiquity nor medievalism either could or would bestow upon it."[29]

In the domain of religion Burckhardt regrets both the failure of Savonarola's reformist preaching and the limited success of the Protestant Reformation, laments the laxity of the faithful and their desertion of the churches, and casts doubt once more on the sincerity of the Christian belief professed by the humanists.

The Christian societies of the Renaissance are nonetheless not wholly deserving of blame in this regard. Burckhardt speaks favorably of the tolerance shown toward Islam and praises the interest taken not only in pagan expressions of religious feeling but also in philosophical movements of antiquity that were incompatible with Christian doctrine, such as Epicureanism. He is especially impressed by the spirit of open-mindedness in entertaining the idea of free will and sees the thinkers of this time as theoreticians and practitioners of an admirable impartiality.

Burckhardt is also alert to the influence exerted by superstition, particularly in its pseudoscientific guise. He notes the spread of astrology and belief in ghosts, demons, witches, and the special kind of sorcery practiced by prostitutes; describes the magical properties associated with laying the foundations of a house or church or city; and notes, by contrast, the diminishing fascination with alchemy. Burckhardt concludes his book with a discussion of the general weakening of faith. Atheism is not yet openly avowed, but theism has plainly yielded to unbelief. The effect of the Renaissance has been to produce a general secularization.

5 | The Renaissance Today

Today, in the early twenty-first century, as during the whole of the century that preceded it, the Renaissance continues to inspire authors who are for the most part, even if sometimes with reservations, inclined to praise it. Their analysis and conclusions may usefully be summarized by briefly considering the work of four exemplary historians: Paul Oskar Kristeller, Eugenio Garin, Erwin Panofsky, and Jean Delumeau.[1]

The first of the four volumes of Paul Oskar Kristeller's influential *Studies in Renaissance Thought and Letters* was published in Rome in 1956. The collection as a whole is concerned chiefly with humanism, but its perspective is considerably broader than this, encompassing in their entirety the literary and artistic productions of what, following Michelet and Burckhardt, Kristeller calls simply the Renaissance. He is also interested in the relationship between this period and the Middle Ages.

A substantial part of the first volume is devoted to one of the great humanists of the fifteenth century, Marsilio Ficino (1433–99), and his role in creating a mode of literary and artistic production that seems not to have existed prior to this time, the circle, consisting of a teacher and his pupils or friends.

It should nevertheless be kept in mind that even if the term *circle* is seldom employed in connection with the Middle Ages, the great writers and painters of this period also gathered around them groups of disciples (often assisted by skilled artisans who were responsible for executing their designs) that strongly resembled the circles of the Renaissance. Just as easel painting gave rise to organized production in studios, so too the medieval workshop brought together wonderfully gifted architects, masons, sculptors, and painters. The principal difference with the studios of the Renaissance is that all these creative minds were closely supervised and directed by the Church.

The staunchest proponents of the view of the Renaissance as an age separate from the medieval period, and superior to it, may be surprised to discover that Kristeller prefaces his account of the great humanist's career with a discussion of his scholastic background. He demonstrates that Ficino's Aristotelianism was directly descended from medieval Aristotelianism, which he had absorbed while studying philosophy at the University of Florence. We should not lose sight of the fact that universities remained a central point of contact between the Middle Ages and the new thinking of the fifteenth century. I shall come back to it in due course.

Kristeller stresses that many humanists had close personal ties to rulers and that they frequently intervened in political matters. It is true that he relies mainly on the situation in Florence to argue this point. The Medicis had gone from banking into politics in the fifteenth century, holding office as citizens of the republic, and then in the sixteenth, after a period of exile, they were restored to power in a princely capacity. They invited humanists to participate in government and claimed themselves to be both political leaders and humanists in their own right. By way of example Kristeller notes the case of Giovanni Corsi, born of a noble family in Florence in 1472. The life of Ficino that Corsi published in 1506 was fulsome in its praise of the Medicis, and after helping them regain power in 1512 he was made a high-ranking diplomat.

The vexed question of the attitude of Renaissance humanists toward Christian belief is taken up with reference to what Ficino described, in a letter of 1474, as a religious conversion, following a period of illness and depression. It must be said that this episode is rather difficult to interpret.

A moment ago I alluded to the Aristotelianism that the Middle Ages bequeathed to the Renaissance. But most Italian humanists of the fourteenth and fifteenth centuries thought of themselves first and foremost as Platonists. The so-called Platonic Academy, founded in Florence around 1440 and dissolved after the death of Lorenzo de' Medici some fifty years later, played a key role in communicating Ficino's ideas. The rediscovery of ancient Greek and Roman thought, and its diffusion from Italy throughout much of Europe, is agreed to be a primary characteristic of the Renaissance. In an article on Lorenzo (the Magnificent, as he was styled) and the Platonistic current of his time, Kristeller insists that "one of the first in whom this tendency clearly appears is Lorenzo de' Medici himself, who was not only Ficino's patron but also a pupil and personal friend. It is therefore necessary to identify the Platonic element in the writings of *il Magnifico*."[2]

In his poems and other works Lorenzo seems to have taken from Plato the definition of love as a desire for beauty, the distinction between heavenly (chaste) love and earthly (physical) love, the tripartite division of beauty (of soul, body, and voice), and the concept of divine beauty as the source of all sensible beauty. His chief interest is the Platonic theory of eternity and the search for true happiness. But for Kristeller it is primarily the concern of Lorenzo and his fellow humanists with the human body that sets the Renaissance apart from the Middle Ages.

It is not the only thing, however. Among the distinctive aspects of the Renaissance mentioned by Kristeller in the papers that make up the second part of this first volume, four seem to me to strengthen the case for treating it as a separate period. The first, the most important of the four in my view, involves the status of man in society and in the universe. Kristeller rightly insists on the need to define the term *humanism*, typically associated with Renaissance men of letters. It has to do, he says, not with man himself, whether in regard to his nature, his existence, or his fate, but with the fact that the great scholars of the age were steeped in what we are used to calling the humanities, that is, the writings of the great thinkers of Greek and Roman antiquity. It was Petrarch in the fourteenth century who inaugurated this form of education, which then spread throughout the various professions of the day. Most humanists were not simply writers or artists. They practiced other trades as well—teaching, for example. Some served as personal secretaries to a prince or worked as town clerks; others were prosperous businessmen or men who held political office. Kristeller holds that Renaissance humanism in this sense had only limited influence, mainly in the curricula of schools and universities, where the classic works of antiquity occupied a considerable place.

Some humanists nevertheless felt confident enough to assert the power of human reason on their own authority. One thinks of another Florentine, Giannozzo Manetti (1396–1459), who wrote a long treatise on the dignity and excellence of man   a reply to the one composed at the very end of the twelfth century by Pope Innocent III (1198–1216) on the misery of the human condition. But we must be careful not to generalize on the basis of such a case, even if Marsilio Ficino was not without successors, Giovanni Pico della Mirandola (1463–94) most notably among them.

A second point advanced by Kristeller in support of the view that the Middle Ages and the Renaissance constitute distinct periods is the legacy of Saint Augustine. Augustine's work, so rich and so susceptible to diverse interpretations, was unrivaled in its importance for medieval thought during virtually every one of its centuries and within every one of its theological and philosophical tendencies. No matter that Augustine had written a treatise entitled *Contra academicos*, he held Plato and Neoplatonism in the highest esteem. Indeed, it was in spite of Augustine's abiding prestige that Aristotelianism managed to achieve a predominant place in medieval thought in the fourteenth and fifteenth centuries. Its influence continued to be felt until the end of the sixteenth, but by that time the humanists, having consulted other ancient authors, had undertaken to read the Fathers of the Church as well. And since they could read Greek, they hastened to translate into Latin, where this had not already been done, the Fathers of the Orthodox Greek Church—Basil, John Chrysostom, Gregory of Nyssa, Cyril, and others.

In the third place Kristeller inquires into the relationship between the thought (and, more generally, the culture) of the Renaissance and music. Surely no one will disagree that early European music enjoyed two moments of incomparable brilliance: the first during the central Middle Ages, in France, with the Notre Dame school and the invention of polyphony; the second, after a lull, in Italy during the fifteenth and still more the sixteenth century.

Fourth, and finally, there is Kristeller's description of the Renaissance festival, a collective celebration of the sort the Middle Ages had likewise known but that later was to be given exceptionally forceful and lively expression, particularly in the courts of nobles and princes. Kristeller bases his account on a hitherto unknown letter, published for the first time in the same article, concerning the joust (*giostra*) organized in Florence by Giuliano de' Medici in 1475. By way of introduction, he says:

Among the public festivals of the Renaissance, jousts occupy a remarkable place. They were numerous and splendid in various Italian cities, particularly Florence, a tradition inherited from the feudal period (perhaps not an insignificant consideration when one wishes to explain the rather belated flowering of chivalric romance in Italy); but in the new environment they took on a quite different aspect, gradually losing their serious and warlike character and becoming transformed into a kind of sporting spectacle in which the spectators' attention was concentrated on the behavior of the combatants, to be sure, but almost more on the solemn entrance of the jousters, richly adorned and forming with their retinue a long motley procession similar to the other parades that were characteristic of public festivals during this time.[3]

The second of the four contemporary historians of the Renaissance I have selected, Eugenio Garin, is remembered for two books in particular, *L'umanesimo italiano* (1947) and *Medioevo e Rinascimento* (1954). In the first of these Garin starts from the rather curious premise that most contemporary historians had revised their opinion of the Middle Ages, which was now regarded more favorably, he says, than it had been in Michelet's and Burckhardt's time, to the disadvantage of the Renaissance. Garin sides instead with Kristeller, calling for the "grand 'cathedrals of ideas'" to be dismantled and with them the "great logico-theological systematisations" that dominated the Middle Ages.[4]

The Renaissance he sees as promoting *studia humanitatis*. Henceforth man occupied center stage: the crushing weight of God on medieval thought and society was now a thing of the past. Platonism became a model and a source of inspiration, a philosophy that was sensitive to problems and nuances. "It was a moral meditation on a life shot through with hope, and it impinged on the borders of mythology. Thus it was a human dialogue, rather than a systematic treatise."[5]

Following in the tradition of Petrarch, who had sought to place the revitalization of intellectual life in the service of government and society, the Platonist movement in Florence considered Cosimo de' Medici (1389–1464), head of the new dominant family, to be a modern Plato. The other great thinker of the Florentine Renaissance, Marsilio Ficino, worshipped at the altar of light, beauty, love, and soul. In pledging allegiance to man rather than God, Ficino and his school naturally came to be identified with what was now called humanism. Garin goes so far as to include Savonarola in this movement, seeing him as a traditionalist whose aim was "to establish on earth a community worthy of man"[6]—a surprising departure from the usual view of Savonarola as the very embodiment of medieval heresy.

In an epilogue Garin emphasizes once more the extent to which the humanism of the Renaissance consisted in "a renewed confidence in man and his possibilities and in an appreciation of man's activity in every possible sense."[7] He also develops two ideas that were to strongly influence subsequent thinking about the relationship between the Middle Ages and the Renaissance: on the one hand, that Italy was the center, the focal point of the Renaissance; on the other, that "the Italy of the Renaissance unite[d] in herself all manner of conflicts."[8]

In *Medioevo e Rinascimento*, an exploration of the Renaissance in its cultural aspect, Garin begins by describing "the crisis of medieval thought."[9] Scholasticism he considers to have exhausted itself by the beginning of the fourteenth century. Even so, he scours the Middle Ages for evidence of both modern traits (the relationship between Abelard and Heloise, for example) and of the rebirth of elements of ancient thought.[10]

Garin dwells at greater length in this work than in the previous one on the new conception of human creativity that emerged during the Renaissance. By conferring on the works of humankind a virtually universal significance, encompassing not only poetry and philology but also moral and political life, the thought of the period amounted to a new philosophy.

The two historians I have just discussed were interested mainly in literature and philosophy—in a word, humanism. The one to whom I now turn, Erwin Panofsky, was one of the foremost art historians of the twentieth century. By itself, the title of his great two-volume work *Renaissance and Renascences in Western Art* (1960) tells us that we are dealing with a different way of looking at the Renaissance than the one with which we are familiar from Kristeller and Garin. Panofsky sees the art of the period as a crucial subject for research and analysis. Most of all, it teaches us to speak of the Renaissance in the plural rather than the singular: there were several "renascences," not just one. These other rebirths ("forerunners" or "precursors," as they are called in the French edition of Panofsky's book) all came before the Renaissance proper.

Panofsky begins by considering, and then dismissing, two tendencies, each widespread in the twentieth century, whose relevance to the question of periodization in history more generally is of particular interest to us: on the one hand, a growing skepticism regarding the very notion of distinct historical periods;[11] on the other, the feeling that "human nature tends to remain much the same in all times."[12] One cannot help but congratulate Panofsky for refusing to take either of these opinions seriously. In effect they deny the possibility of doing history, the one partially, the other completely.

Like those who regard the Renaissance as a period in its own right, Panofsky goes back to Petrarch and the idea that the revival of Greek and Roman literature was a kind of cleansing. Little more than a century after the poet's death, the narrow identification of the Renaissance with literature and philosophy had given way to a broader perspective. By 1500 or so, he says, "the concept of [a] great revival had come to include nearly all fields of cultural endeavor."[13]

Panofsky also quotes the philosopher George Boas, who argued that "what we call 'periods' are simply the names of the influential innovations which have occurred constantly in . . . history."[14] On this view historical periods should bear the name of a great figure: the age of Beethoven, for example, just as it was once common to speak of the age of Pericles or the age of Louis XIV.[15]

Panofsky goes on to criticize the very influential argument developed by the painter and historian of art Giorgio Vasari, who worked in Florence in the sixteenth century, in *Le vite de' più eccel-lenti architetti, pittori e scultori italiani* (Lives of the Most Eminent Architects, Painters, and Sculptors, 1550), dedicated to Cosimo de' Medici. Vasari considered that with Giotto (ca. 1266–1337), which is to say from the beginning of the fourteenth century, there began a new period of humanity, which he called the Renaissance (*Rinas-cita*), whose chief motive force was a desire to revive the learning of classical antiquity. Panofsky remarks that scholars today have a more nuanced idea of the Renaissance than its leading artistic, literary, and political figures did, at least in Italy: infatuated with the notion of a return to the glories of Greece and Rome, which they saw as an ideal age, these elites could not help but regard its successor, now more and more commonly thought of as an inter-mediate period, as an age of decline.

Two works by another great historian, Jean Delumeau, will con-clude this brief sketch of recent thinking. In the first, *La Renais-sance* (1996),[16] Delumeau notes the dual emergence of the usual name for this period. The name, and the idea of renewal through a return to antiquity it implies, were first encountered in Italy, and in particular in Florence. It was introduced by Petrarch in the mid-fourteenth century and then given a more general meaning by Vasari in the mid-sixteenth century. But, as we have seen, the name, and the period that is now associated with it, did not come to be widely accepted until the nineteenth century, with Michelet and the romantic movement. The Renaissance, in other words, over time acquired a broader significance, which went beyond the domain of the arts to refer to the principal aspects of a period extending from the dark Middle Ages until the luminous modern age, whose advent it announced.

In the second work, a history of the Renaissance published three years later, Delumeau begins by describing the spread of a new style of art, first from Florence through the rest of Italy, then from Italy through the rest of Europe.[17] He notes a splendid anomaly: the great Dutch painter Pieter Brueghel the Elder (ca. 1527–69), who knew nothing of either antiquity or Italy.

Delumeau looks next at developments in humanistic education and artistic training: the diffusion of printing, the growing number of schools, the decline of universities and the rise of courts, the new prominence of authors and learned women; the appearance of a new form of instruction, the studio, associated chiefly with oil painting, and the vogue for easel painting, invented in the Netherlands in the fifteenth century; the emergence of scholarly societies, which recreated in a new form what in antiquity was meant by the Greek term *academy*. Among the many examples of technological advance that Delumeau attributes to the Renaissance, he cites in particular the mechanical clock and artillery. For my part I consider them to have been medieval inventions. The Renaissance was also characterized in his view by its economic dynamism. This seems to me an exaggeration. There were nonetheless two novelties of unarguable importance: the stockpiling of precious metals (gold and silver) brought back from America, where they had been discovered at the very end of the fifteenth century and the beginning of the sixteenth; and the improvement of techniques of maritime navigation, stimulated by the voyages of Christopher Columbus and the caravels of the late Middle Ages. I shall come back to these things later.

Daily life, now shaped to a rather considerable degree by the annual recurrence of various festivals, is accorded its own chapter. A new atmosphere came into being, the result of a growing taste for luxury and entertainments in princely courts, sometimes even among prosperous merchants and urban notables.[18] Finally, a crowning touch, Delumeau treats modernity in ecclesiastical affairs as an aspect of what he calls great religious transformations. Here, of course, he has in mind the Reformation and the birth of a separate branch of Christianity—Protestantism, in each of its two principal forms, Lutheranism and Calvinism. Evidently this was experienced as a major change in the lives of the men and women of the time, in which atheism was still seldom expressed openly.

Delumeau concludes by looking back over the Renaissance as a whole. Although he acknowledges its limitations, he nonetheless considers it to have marked a great step forward. He justifies this view by appeal to literary and artistic works that he sees as having set new standards of excellence. But what sets the Renaissance entirely apart from the era preceding it are two great moments that changed the course of history: the discovery of America and the successful circumnavigation of the globe, on the one hand, and the splitting of Western Christianity into two branches, Catholicism and Protestantism, on the other.

The time has now come for me to argue on behalf of two propositions of my own. First, as important as the Renaissance undoubtedly was, and however reasonable it may seem to mark it off as a discrete segment of historical time, I do not believe that the Renaissance can truly be said to constitute a separate period. It seems to me instead to constitute the last renaissance of a long Middle Ages. I should also like to show that periodization remains an indispensable principle for the historian, even if the globalization of culture and the decentering of the West we witness today have caused its legitimacy to be challenged. Just the same, it must be used with greater flexibility than it has been until now.

6 | The Middle Ages Become the Dark Ages

The hostility toward the Middle Ages, indeed the contempt for it that was felt and often expressed by cultural elites during the Renaissance, beginning in the fourteenth century but increasingly during the fifteenth and, above all, in the sixteenth century, was further intensified in the eighteenth century by the anticlerical bias of Enlightenment thinkers. This condemnation was based primarily, as we have seen, on a perceived need to go back to the leading lights of classical antiquity (Aristotle and Plato in Greece, Cicero and Seneca in Rome), whom medieval scholars were said to have ignored in constructing their vast cathedrals of the mind.

Greco-Roman culture did pose a problem for medievals from the religious point of view, of course, for the ancients were "pagans." But not only did they not ignore its existence or fail to appreciate its value; they often drew from it—so much so that they may be said to have carried on classical tradition in their own way. This ambivalence was inevitable once they made Saint Augustine, a man of Roman education who had converted to Christianity, their great teacher. It was on the basis of the classical system of liberal arts that rational, scientific, and pedagogical thinking developed in the Middle Ages until the thirteenth century, when it began to be superseded by the instruction given in universities.

A succession of magisterial figures transmitted this system from antiquity to the Middle Ages. The first was Varro (116–27 BCE), appointed by Julius Caesar to oversee the first public library in Rome, who distinguished the liberal arts from the mechanical, manual arts. In the Middle Ages this distinction was to stimulate debate in religious and intellectual circles about the significance of labor, from both a theoretical and a practical point of view.

Study of the liberal arts received fresh impetus in late antiquity from a poem by the fifth-century author Martianus Capella, *De nuptiis philologiae et mercurii* (On the Marriage of Philology and Mercury), an essential text in the centuries that followed. Two great thinkers, Cassiodorus (sixth century) and Alcuin (a member of Charlemagne's court in the late eighth to early ninth century), were largely responsible for the division of the seven liberal arts into two branches: the *trivium*, concerned with the study of words, which is to say grammar, rhetoric, and dialectic; and the *quadrivium*, comprising arithmetic, geometry, music, and astronomy.

In carrying on the tradition of ancient Rome, the Middle Ages brought about a major cultural advance as well: the use of Latin by scholars and secular elites in all the areas of Europe that had been Christianized. Naturally this language differed from classical Latin.

It nevertheless formed the basis for long-lasting linguistic unity in Europe, extending even beyond the twelfth and thirteenth centuries, when vernacular languages (such as French) began to replace an outmoded form of daily communication, especially among the lower classes of society. The Middle Ages were, all things considered, a much more Latinized period than the Renaissance.

Reading and writing were more common during the Middle Ages than in antiquity. Schooling, for girls as well as boys, became more widely available. The growing adoption of parchment, easier to handle than papyrus, and, more important still, the method of producing books by stacking and binding sheets in a form known as the *codex*, which by the fourth or fifth century had superseded the roll (*volumen*), encouraged the spread of literacy as well. As for writing, it is true that the medieval *scriptores* did not manage to unify the various extant styles of lettering. One of the signal successes of the Renaissance was that it established a dominant style for humanistic calligraphy, first popularized by Petrarch and thereafter called "roman." Another one of the Renaissance's great achievements by comparison with the Middle Ages was the rediscovery of ancient Greek in the major centers of Western Christendom, aided by the exile of Byzantine scholars after the taking of Constantinople by the Turks in 1453.

Between the fifteenth century and the end of the eighteenth, the impression grew that the plunge into darkness thought to have occurred during the medieval period was accompanied by a retreat from reason into the realm of the passions, ruled by the miraculous and the supernatural. But most scholars during the

Middle Ages, and the system of education they expounded in universities and schools, made almost constant reference to reason (*ratio*) in each of its two senses: ordered thought and calculation. To the medieval mind, rationality was what distinguished human from animal nature. The supremacy of reason is encountered in both Augustine and Boethius. In the thirteenth century, eminent scholastics such as Albert the Great and Thomas Aquinas borrowed from the *Book of Definitions* by Isaac Israeli (c. 855–955) the idea that "reason is born in the shadow of intelligence."[1] In theology, reason was opposed to authority. It is true, however, that the quite formalistic conception of reason in the Middle Ages put obstacles in the way of the development of scientific rationality that were not removed until the Renaissance.

The Dominican scholar Marie-Dominique Chenu showed how rationality came increasingly to be introduced into theology, transforming it into something like a science in the thirteenth century.[2] As far as scholasticism is concerned, Nicolas Weill-Parot has demonstrated in a recent work the "profound rationality of scholastic scientific thought in the Middle Ages."[3]

Let us now consider the question in its geographic aspect. It was in Italy, as I say, that the movement that later was to be called the Renaissance began. A more detailed study than the present one would call attention to the role played by this or that city, Genoa, Florence, Pisa, or Venice. The main thing that needs to be kept in mind is that Italy as a whole seemed to announce a new historical age. From the point of view of periodization, Italy is, if I may put it this way, a troublemaker.

In antiquity Italy distinguished itself through the power of the Etruscans and, above all, of the Roman Empire. During the Middle Ages it was very divided politically in the aftermath of the pope's exile to Avignon in the fifteenth century, and it compensated for its weaknesses through an exceptional artistic flowering, most notably in Florence and Venice. Girolamo Arnaldi has shown that from the early Middle Ages onward, though it was always dominated by foreigners, wholly or partially, Italy remained a beacon of light for all of Europe, beginning with its own invaders.[4]

Similarly, in the fifteenth and sixteenth centuries, the artistic and cultural radiance of the Renaissance emanated in the first place from Italy, although Germany, particularly in the south, was not slow to follow its example and displayed considerable originality of its own.[5]

The urge to periodize obliges the historian to take into account the dominant mode of thought in a given age, over as wide a geographic area as possible. The Middle Ages began on a pessimistic note. The periodization that the Christian Church caused to prevail was due to Augustine, in which the world is to know six ages—the sixth, the last, being the one during which humanity awaits the eternity that will follow the Last Judgment. The accepted formula, as we saw earlier, was *mundus senescit* (the world grows old). From this, as chronicles and sermons testify, came the idea of decay. The world was nearing not its salvation but its final ruin.

This idea was soon challenged, however, by a number of monastic scholars who argued that their contemporaries should see themselves as moderns (*moderni*) rather than as ancients.

Without insisting on the absolute superiority of their own age, they praised its qualities and spoke of a fresh outlook on the world. They regarded the Middle Ages as a new time. In the clashes between past, present, and future that were to follow, it was the claim to just this, modernity, that was really being contested.

Toward the end of his career the historian of medieval philosophy Étienne Gilson published a short essay called "The Middle Ages as *saeculum modernum*."[6] Since people in the Middle Ages were unaware that their era would one day be known by this name, Gilson wondered how they saw it themselves, taking a long view— the long view of history as it was written down by the chroniclers and also as it was remembered then by most men and women. Now, scholars supposed that the age of the ancients had continued up until Charlemagne. For the times that came after, they imagined that a transfer of learning (*translatio studii*) had taken place from ancient Greece and Rome to the West, and more particularly Gaul. The eleventh century was thought to mark a break from antiquity, with grammar being replaced by logic as the major art of the *trivium*—a modest prelude to the triumph of science over letters. In the latter part of that century, under the influence of Anselm of Canterbury, *eloquentia* gave way to *dialectica* as an intellectual ideal; the logic of Aristotle began to be studied, and scholasticism was called "modern."

Gilson hastens to add that the concept of modernity was apt to be interpreted by conservative thinkers in a pejorative sense. Thus, at the beginning of the twelfth century, Guibert de Nogent spoke in his autobiography of the corruption that the modern age introduced in both thought and morality. The turning point, the moment when the new era could be said to have undoubtedly established itself, came with the appearance of John of Salisbury's *Metalogicon* (1159). "Novelty was introduced everywhere," John says, "with innovations in grammar, changes in dialectic, rhetoric declared irrelevant, and the rules of previous teachers expelled from the very sanctuary of philosophy to make way for the promulgation of new systems throughout the *quadrivium*."[7]

In the fourteenth century an impassioned campaign aimed at reforming the Church was undertaken by the Flemish scholar and preacher Gerard Groote (1340–84), who urged that Christian spirituality be brought into closer alignment with Christ's own example. This movement, whose various tendencies were to be embodied in the sixteenth century by the founder of the Jesuits, Ignatius of Loyola, became known as *devotio moderna* so widely, in fact, that the earliest exponents of what was to be called the Renaissance denigrated the modernity of the Middle Ages. Thus the urging of the fifteenth-century Florentine architect Antonio di Pietro Averlino, known as Filarete, in his *Trattato di architettura* (1460–64): "I therefore call upon everyone to renounce modern habits and to disregard the counsels of the masters who practice this vulgar system."[8]

Indeed, historians consider the principal expression of *devotio moderna*, the *De imitatione Christi* attributed to Thomas à Kempis (c. 1380–1471), to be the great masterpiece of pre-Renaissance religious literature. In allying the obligation of Christians to study the Bible with a concern for reforming the Church, it stressed the importance of cultivating personal spirituality through the union of action and contemplation—what Ignatius of Loyola was to call discernment (*discretio*).

From all of this the awkwardness of appealing to *modernity*, a term of approval and disparagement alike, will be evident. Plainly it cannot serve as a criterion for detecting historical change of the sort that was later to be identified with "progress." It was in the twelfth century, after all, that the renovators of theological and philosophical thought became fond of quoting the Neoplatonist philosopher Bernard of Chartres (died c. 1124): "We are like dwarfs sitting on the shoulders of giants so that we are able to see more and further than they, not indeed by reason of the sharpness of our own vision or the height of our bodies, but because we are lifted up on high and raised aloft by the greatness of giants."[9]

As against what they objected to as scholastic obscurantism, the learned men of the Renaissance proposed a system of intellectual and cultural training based on *studia humanitatis*, which we have come to refer to as the humanities. But this way of conceiving of education was much older than is generally supposed: it marks off what was to be called the Middle Ages no less than what was to be called the Renaissance.

With regard to the sort of humanism associated with Bernard of Chartres, I take the liberty of quoting from one of my own writings, itself inspired by the suggestive insights of Fr. Chenu, for whom this style dominated the theology of the twelfth century: "Man was the object and the center of creation. This is the import of the *Cur Deus homo* controversy: Why did God become man?"[10]

Taking issue with the traditional thesis put forward by Saint Gregory, that human beings are an accident of creation—an *ersatz*, a substitute, fortuitously created by God to replace the rebellious angels that had been cast out of heaven—and elaborating on an argument by Saint Anselm, Bernard held that man had always been a part of the Creator's plan, indeed, that it was for man that the world was made. One of the greatest theologians of the twelfth century, Honorius of Autun, trained in Anselm's school at Canterbury, in England, likewise insisted that "this world was created for man."[11] Man was a rational being before all else. This rationalism might well be called humanistic, except that man is understood to absorb the world around him and, in so doing, to become an active and meaningful summary of it. It is this image of humanity as microcosm that one encounters in the writings of Bernard Silvestris (active twelfth century) and Alain de Lille (1128–1203), as well as in many miniatures, such as the one in the celebrated Lucca manuscript of the *Liber divinorum operum* by Hildegard of Bingen.

The intellectual renaissance of the twelfth century is probably best characterized by the school of Saint Victor, established by a group of theologians (known as the Victorines, after one of their number, Hugues de Saint-Victor) at the edge of the medieval city of Paris (a rue Saint-Victor still exists today in the fifth arrondissement). Hugues himself, who died in 1141, compiled a collection of theological and philosophical readings, the *Didascalicon de studio legendi*; composed a treatise on the sacraments, *De sacramentis christianae fidei*, one of the first theological summas of the Middle Ages; and wrote, among other works, a commentary on Pseudo-Dionysius that was later to be incorporated as part of the curriculum of the University of Paris in the thirteenth century, thus helping to prolong the renaissance of the twelfth century. Inclined by temperament to contemplation, and committed to the revival of the liberal arts and, more generally, the thought of antiquity, Saint-Victor well deserved the epithet "the new Augustine."

Here I should emphasize that if the seventeenth century rather discreetly preserved the idea of a renaissance during the Middle Ages as a sort of gray area, without either criticizing it or treating it with contempt, it nevertheless was pleased to rescue from obscurity a few figures whose memory was be celebrated by association with a particular state or family or place long after their death. One thinks of King Louis IX of France (d. 1270). Canonized by the Church, patron saint of the royal family (most notably of Louis XIII and, more famously still, Louis XIV), his glory was carried across the seas to places where the French had settled: to Africa, where the first French trading post was established as Saint-Louis du Sénégal in 1638 or so under Louis XIII; later to North America, where the city of Saint Louis was founded at the confluence of the Missouri and Mississippi Rivers in 1764. In the meantime the Royal and Military Order of Saint Louis was created by Louis XIV in 1693, abolished by the Revolution in 1793, reestablished by the Bourbons in 1814, and finally dissolved once and for all with the abdication of Charles X in 1830. As for the Île

Saint-Louis in Paris, it received its name in 1627, the result of join-
ing together two small islands in the Seine.

Scholastic philosophy (so called because it was often taught in
schools, which is to say universities) was the main focus of the
criticism—indeed, the rejection—of the Middle Ages by the
learned men of the sixteenth century to begin with, and later,
even more forcefully, by the philosophers of the eighteenth century. The term *scholastic*, introduced as an adjective in the thirteenth century, was used from the sixteenth century onward to
refer to a style of medieval thought that was strongly influenced
by theology. Voltaire went so far as to say: "Scholastic theology,
the bastard offspring of Aristotelian philosophy, poorly translated
and misunderstood, did more to harm reason and proper education than the Huns and the Vandals did."[12]

Medieval thought underwent a kind of rehabilitation in the
nineteenth century. Even so, one still encountered opinions such
as the one Ernest Renan expressed in his *Vie de Jésus* (1863): "It
is characteristic of scholastic education that it closed the mind to
everything fine."[13] This was a more subtle formulation than Voltaire's, perhaps, but the verdict remained the same: the men and
women of the Middle Ages were barbarians.

I need hardly say that the Middle Ages were a profoundly
religious epoch, marked by the power of the Church, which was
itself the expression of an almost universal piety. The sixteenth
century was, of course, a momentous time, bringing about the
Reformation and, in its train, fierce and protracted religious

wars. Christian faith henceforth appeared in at least two forms, the traditional Catholic version and the new revised one, also called Protestant, which comprised several orientations: in Great Britain, Anglicanism; on the continent, Lutheranism and Calvinism, the former taking root mainly in the Germanic and Nordic regions, the latter in those where Romance languages were spoken. But it was still in any case a matter of *Christian* faith. Only in the seventeenth century did there emerge a group of scholarly unbelievers, known as libertines. A well-known early example was Pierre Gassendi (1592–1655), philosopher and professor of mathematics at the Collège de France. Libertines appear in Molière's *Tartuffe* (1664) and *Don Juan* (1665), but the Académie française recognized their name only in the fourth edition of its dictionary a century later, in 1762.

If there is one domain in which the novelty of the Renaissance seems undeniable, it is art. Probably the most important departure from the past came with the birth of a modern conception of beauty. Yet it was in the Middle Ages, not the Renaissance, that it occurred. Umberto Eco demonstrated this more than fifty years ago in a remarkable essay, "Sviluppo dell'estetica medievale."[14] One of the principal accusations brought against the Middle Ages by Renaissance thinkers, Eco points out, was that the period lacked an "aesthetic sensibility."[15] Vigorously disputing the notion that scholasticism had smothered all sense of beauty, he shows that medieval theology and philosophy took a keen interest in aesthetic questions. He does not consider particular works but rather the concern with beauty itself. Anyone who has read and reflected on Henri Focillon's writing on medieval art, in *L'art des sculpteurs romans* (1931) and, especially, *Art d'Occident* (1938),[16] will be no less persuaded, contemplating a Romanesque church or a Gothic cathedral, not only that this age produced artistic masterpieces but that it was moved by a profound sense of beauty—and by an equally profound desire to give it a physical expression that could be offered to God and to humankind. Indeed, the Middle Ages produced an abundance of masterpieces. Not the least of these were illuminated manuscripts, works of art that by their very nature few people could see.

The Middle Ages also created the artist. He was no longer simply an artisan, someone skilled in manual work. He was now inspired by the desire to produce something beautiful and devoted his life to doing just this. He practiced something more than a trade, nearer to a destiny, and came to acquire in medieval society a prestige that the architects, painters, and sculptors of the early Middle Ages, anonymous for the most part, did not enjoy. Moreover, those who succeeded in creating a name for themselves could make a living mainly from their work. With the increasingly widespread use of money in the thirteenth and fourteenth centuries, these men joined a class of people who now found themselves at the pinnacle of society: the wealthy.

The first person who was acknowledged by his own contemporaries to be an artist was Giotto. He was based in Florence, probably the most prosperous and the most beautiful city in Italy at the turn of the fourteenth century. It was also at the forefront of a new aesthetic movement. Giotto first attracted notice with a cycle of frescoes in Assisi, depicting the life of St. Francis, and another in the Basilica of the Holy Cross in Florence. But his reputation as an artist seems to date from his decoration of the Scrovegni Chapel in Padua, completed around 1305.

In the domain of religious architecture there was no major change in the Middle Ages, apart, of course, from the eclipse of the Romanesque style by what Alain Erlande-Brandenburg has called the "Gothic revolution of the twelfth century."[17] But financial crises, the economic consequences of the plague, and wars had the effect in combination of drying up sources of funding for cathedrals and caused some of them to be left unfinished, most notably in Siena.

In the domain of secular architecture, by contrast, a profound transformation was under way. Until the fourteenth century the fortified seigneurial castle was, above all, a place of refuge in times of danger. But with the development of cannon, now more and more frequently used in combat, even castles offered little protection, and rather quickly they were converted from their original military purpose into grand country estates. Particular attention was paid to the design of staircases, furnishings, and promenades.

As for painting, while credit for the appearance in Flanders in the mid-fifteenth century of oil painting and easel painting cannot be ascribed with confidence to the Middle Ages, rather than the Renaissance, one crucial innovation was indisputably medieval: the personal portrait. It is on account of a novel interest in producing close likenesses, often by drawing from life, that a great many carefully observed images of the men and women of that time have come down to us today. The really decisive advance, however, sprang from the importance that was now attached to the individual. To be sure, the medieval portrait was typically a picture of a person's face. But the face is a part of the body, and it was the body that was to conquer historical memory from this point on.

Gerhart B. Ladner, a great historian of Renaissance art, argued that a distinctive characteristic of the art of this era, by contrast with the medieval period, was the generous place it accorded to vegetation.[18] It is true that plant life had mainly a symbolic sense. But its luxuriance is enough by itself, in Ladner's eyes, to illustrate the concept of rebirth, which made the Renaissance a kind of springtime of the world after the winter of the Middle Ages.

And yet the Middle Ages were filled with flowers and leaves and trees as well. Almost everyone had the sense of having been born with Adam and Eve in the Garden of Eden and, in a way, of never having left it. Original sin did, of course, deprive humanity of the carefree enjoyment of this happy world. But in obliging men and women to labor in the fields, it gave them not only food but also beauty—and, along with it, a glimpse of heaven.

In their recent book on the Romanesque world, Jérôme Baschet, Jean-Claude Bonne, and Pierre-Olivier Dittmar devote a whole chapter to "vegetality."[19] Here again we are dealing mainly with a symbolic world. But earthly vegetation was not neglected. In this as in other domains, the Renaissance only prolonged the Middle Ages, opening up to humanity a closed garden, the symbol of Mary's virginity:

A garden enclosed, my sister, my bride,
a spring closed off, a fountain sealed!
Your branches are a grove of pomegranates
with fruits of choicest yield:
henna with spikenard.[20]

The greatest literary masterpiece of the Middle Ages, Dante's *Divine Comedy*, burgeons and blossoms once Beatrice leaves Purgatory for Paradise; one of the most popular allegorical poems (or romances) of the thirteenth century, *Le roman de la rose*, has a flower as its object and unfolds in a symbolic expanse of vegetation.

I should mention in passing here that the history of music leads us to see the Renaissance in a different light as well. Some years ago the sociologist Norbert Elias wrote a remarkable book on the figure and career of Wolfgang Amadeus Mozart (1756–91).[21] Elias shows that during the years 1781 and 1782 Mozart was able to achieve independence as a composer and performer by freeing himself from the domination of an overbearing father and an artistically stifling subservience to his first employers, the archbishop of Salzburg and the emperor of Austria. In the person of Mozart the individual had thus managed at last to assert himself—an essential moment that marks the passing of a long Middle Ages and the entry into the modern era.

At the juncture of the Middle Ages and the Renaissance there developed a practice that provoked trepidation and tumult in the Church and in Christian society: sorcery, specifically in the form of witchcraft. Two points need to be clarified before we begin. First,

Michelet located the spread of witchcraft in the fourteenth century, but reliance on a doubtful source led him into error. In fact, it began in the fifteenth century. Second, witchcraft was essentially a phenomenon involving women and had a great impact on the opinion of society about women, with the result that they were not objects of respect and admiration during the Renaissance, as tradition would have it; instead, they were feared and despised on the whole, regarded as ambiguous creatures, part divine, part diabolical.

The term *sorcerer* seems first to have appeared in the twelfth century. It took on its full meaning from the moment when Thomas Aquinas, in his *Summa theologica* (second half of the thirteenth century), famously defined a sorcerer as someone who has made a pact with the devil. It was altogether natural, then, that two centuries later, witches should have come to be seen as satanic figures. Before long their mythical iconography was settled: a woman traveling across the sky astride a broom or a stick.

It is therefore more accurate to say that the witch is an emblem of the Renaissance, even of the classical age, rather than of the Middle Ages. To the extent that the Middle Ages did play a role in the creation of this image, it is with regard to a widespread anxiety about witchcraft, aggravated around 1260 when Pope Alexander IV instructed inquisitors to investigate charges of sorcery where heresy was involved, so that witches were now liable to be put to death by burning. It was in the context of a new popular mentality, and of a new attitude on the part of the Church, that Aquinas introduced the idea of a pact with the devil. The fifteenth century was to make the gloom of this dark time complete by adding participation in a witches' Sabbath to the list of crimes punishable by torture and death. Surely the most familiar episode of brutal suppression occurred in the early 1630s, in France, in the aftermath of unrest among the Ursulines of Loudun, which ended with the priest Urbain Grandier (1590–1634) being sentenced to death at the stake.

But it was in the late fifteenth century, when the Renaissance was already well under way, according to its advocates, that two German Dominicans, Heinrich Kramer and Jakob Sprenger, published an immensely influential handbook of repressive violence under the title *Malleus maleficarum* (The Hammer of Witches, 1486). Jean-Patrice Boudet, noting that witches at this time were often called "Waldenses" (an epidemic of Waldensian heresy had broken out in the northern French town of Arras in 1459–60), argues that the enthusiastic response to Kramer and Sprenger's work had been prepared some years earlier by debate at the Councils of Constance (1414–18) and, especially, of Basel (1431–49).[22] The French monarchy, for its part, had expanded the definition of the crime of lèse majesté to include witchcraft. It seems not unreasonable, then, to suggest that the phenomenon of witchcraft may be associated with a certain political periodization. I shall come back to this point later.

In the meantime let me conclude the present discussion by briefly considering a recent book about the Renaissance in relation to the modern age that I mentioned earlier, by Robert C. Davis and Beth Lindsmith. They begin by drawing a stark contrast between the Middle Ages and the Renaissance that brings out the novel character of this latter period: "Half a millennium after lighting up Europe's cultural landscape, the Renaissance still evokes the springtime of Modernity, when medieval fears and follies were discarded for new hope."[23]

Davis and Lindsmith agree that the new spirit arose in Italy and that in about 1500 it began to spread throughout Europe. Once again we encounter an emphasis on Italy's special geographic and cultural significance in the history of periodization. Yet they go on at once, if not to contradict themselves, then at least to undermine their initial claim: "Like the humans who made it, however, Europe's time of rebirth also had its dark side." Implicitly recalling the publication of the *Malleus maleficarum* in the late fifteenth century, they are forced to concede at the very outset: "Pogroms, the Inquisition and millenarian religious movements all flourished more vigorously [during the Renaissance] than they had during the Middle Ages."[24]

Plainly there was a time of coexistence, and sometimes a tension, between a late Middle Ages that extended into the sixteenth century and an early Renaissance that first made its presence felt at the beginning of the fifteenth century. In the next chapter I shall return to the question of transitional moments, or turning points. For the moment, however, let us look more closely at this particular time, when the Middle Ages and the Renaissance overlapped.

Patrick Boucheron, in his introduction to a recent volume of papers on world history during the fifteenth century, shows that in the absence of any sort of global unity there was only interaction among what he calls "territories."[25] The heart of the European territory, leaving to one side the marginal areas of the Mediterranean and the Iberian Peninsula, presents two aspects of particular interest: on the one hand, what Pierre Monnet calls "an empire of crowns"[26] and, on the other, the rise of the modern state, examined separately by Jean-Philippe Genet.[27]

Genet argues for the decisive importance of linguistic change: Latin was reduced in the fourteenth century to the status of a scholarly language, having been replaced in daily life by national languages. Alongside the nation, the state became established mainly through taxation.

From all of this, it seems to me, one critical implication emerges concerning the periodization of history. True discontinuities are rare. Ruptures in the strict sense, clean breaks with what went before, are seldom observed. The usual case is the more or less long, the more or less profound transformation: the turning point, the internal renaissance.

7 | A Long Middle Ages

What I must now try to show, with regard not only to culture but also to economics, politics, and social relations, is that no fundamental changes occurred in the sixteenth century, nor indeed at any time before the middle of the eighteenth century, that would justify our marking off the Middle Ages from a new and different period, the Renaissance.

At the end of the fifteenth century, of course, there did occur an event of very great consequence for Europe: the discovery by Columbus of what he took to be the East Indies but which turned out to be a new continent, soon to be called America. The Western world's horizons were broadened further early in the sixteenth century with Magellan's circling of the globe. But it was only in the late eighteenth century that the larger repercussions of these discoveries began to be felt. North America cannot truly be said to have made its entrance on the international stage until the founding of the United States in 1776, nor South America before the liberation by Simón Bolívar from 1810 onward of most of the Spanish colonial states.

The development of deep-sea navigation—more important perhaps than European colonization, which really gathered momentum only after the middle of the eighteenth century, and more particularly in the nineteenth century—can be traced to the Middle Ages. The high seas were opened up to Europeans by the introduction in the thirteenth century of the compass, the sternpost rudder, and the square sail. Henceforth the northern countries of Europe were able to communicate with the Mediterranean by means of boats carrying not only merchandise but also people. The first regularly scheduled commercial voyage, from Genoa to Bruges, took place in 1297. Fernand Braudel reminds us that "Lisbon's rise in the thirteenth century was that of a port of call which gradually assimilated the lessons of an active, maritime, peripheral, and capitalist economy."[1] Later I shall take issue with the use of the term *capitalist* in this context. For the moment it is enough to emphasize that an activity of major historical importance, in large part maritime, that is usually said to have begun only in the fifteenth or sixteenth century had, in fact, a medieval origin.

And yet high-speed transport by water or (in the case of horse-drawn coaches) by land was nevertheless very slow. Not until the eighteenth century did improved highways make overland travel in France safer and more rapid. With the construction of well-paved main roads, the "lease of the French posts rose from 1,220,000 livres in 1676 to 8,800,000 in 1776," Braudel observes. "The budget of the *Ponts et Chaussées* department was 700,000 under Louis XIV and 7 million as the Revolution drew near."[2] The École des ponts et chaussées, for its part, was founded in 1747.

I turn now to the economic dimension of the Renaissance in Europe. Alain Tallon has observed that the European economy during this period never managed to overcome "the weakness that is inherent in every system of traditional production: in the absence of any real changes in the methods of cultivation employed almost everywhere, and therefore of any significant increase in agricultural yields, [the economy] was incapable of growth."[3]

European agriculture did undergo a certain degree of development during the Middle Ages. The invention of the iron plowshare allowed deeper furrows to be cut; the adoption of a new plan of crop rotation meant that a third of the fields under cultivation was left fallow each year, rather than half; and the replacement of the ox by the horse as the principal draft animal increased productivity in addition to yields. But a rural economy that in other respects had remained essentially unchanged for centuries survived until the 1500s. Indeed, the traditional system became stronger since profits generated by commerce and the nascent institution of banking were typically reinvested in landholding. This was true in Italy with the *banchieri* of Genoa and Florence, and in France with the *grands officiers de finance* under Francis I.[4]

Another element of continuity between the Middle Ages and the Renaissance is the development of economic thought. Its birth may be said to have coincided with the first use of the term *value* in a theoretical sense, by the great scholastic philosopher Albert the

Great in his translation of Aristotle's *Nicomachean Ethics* around 1250. As Sylvain Piron has convincingly argued, it was owing to the *Tractatus de contractibus* (c. 1292) of the heretical Franciscan theologian Pierre de Jean Olivi that economic analysis was able to take a major step forward. Many of the notions introduced in this work, such as "scarcity," "capital," and "usury," subsequently became objects of lively theoretical and practical debate.[5] The prohibition of usury, which is to say lending at interest, reached its height with the decree by Pope Urbain III around 1187, then gradually disappeared, apparently not later than the eighteenth century (there is no mention of it in Napoleon's civil code of 1804). In 1615 a treatise by Antoine de Montchrestien (1575–1621) proposed the novel concept of political economy (*économie politique*). Until then, *economy* had referred to household management, its original sense in Aristotle and other ancient Greek authors. Capitalism in the West was the result of a long process of evolution whose economic and social foundations were evidently undisturbed by any rupture the Renaissance might have brought about.

Fernand Braudel's great book *Civilisation matérielle et capitalisme, XVe–XVIIIe siècles* (1967) is an invaluable resource for anyone interested in estimating the degree of continuity between the Middle Ages and the Renaissance.[6] In the rural world of an *ancien régime* that held sway in Europe from the turn of the twelfth century until the eve of the French Revolution, harvests alternated with famines. France, which Braudel considers to have been a privileged country in this respect, experienced ten general famines in the tenth century, twenty-six in the eleventh, two in the twelfth, four in the fourteenth, seven in the fifteenth, thirteen in the sixteenth, eleven in the seventeenth, and sixteen in the eighteenth.[7] Plague, the most terrible of all epidemics, ravaged Europe repeatedly between 1348 and 1720; neither the fifteenth nor the sixteenth century can really be said to have constituted a departure from this pattern.

Braudel further emphasizes that, until the eighteenth century in Europe, nourishment was derived mainly from vegetables and cereal grains.[8] It is a curiosity that in France, long a nation of carnivores, the share of meat in the average person's diet did not increase during the sixteenth century, which the advocates of the Renaissance look upon as an age of prosperity. To the contrary, the quantities of meat consumed after 1550 fell drastically. Demand for beverages and vegetables imported from regions outside Europe from the sixteenth century onward was limited. This was true not only of chocolate and tea (the latter being favored chiefly in Great Britain, the Low Countries, and Russia) but also of coffee (which reached Europe in the mid-seventeenth century but did not really become popular until the second half of the eighteenth, and even then mostly in southern and central Europe). Yields for wheat (or rather wheats—mixed crops of wheat and rye, for example), remained low until the eighteenth century; fertilizer was obtained from humans and animals. Food shortages in the summer of 1789 were surely not the least of the causes of the unrest that led to the Revolution in France.

Beginning in the twelfth century, as more and more mills were put into operation, bread production increased to the point that it soon formed the basis of nutrition throughout Europe. Price varied as a function of quality, and a visible difference appeared between the bread of the peasants, which was almost black, and the virtually white bread of the bourgeoisie and nobility. As Braudel observes, however, the "real revolution in white bread only occurred between 1750 and 1850. At that period wheat took the place of other cereals (as in England) and bread was increasingly made from flours that had had most of the bran removed."[9]

The upper classes began to demand better food, better from the point of view both of taste and health. Fermented bread was increasingly preferred as an alternative to gruel, traditionally the foundation of the French diet (Diderot, for example, found it indigestible). A school devoted to baking, the École nationale de boulangerie, was founded in 1780, and shortly afterward "Napoleon's soldiers introduced this 'precious commodity, white bread' all over Europe."[10]

Fishing off the northern coasts, together with new techniques for preserving fish, made herring a staple food throughout the Continent. From the eleventh century onward the great herring fisheries of the Baltic and North Seas made fishermen from the Hanse wealthy and, later, fishermen from Holland and Zealand as well. Around 1350 a Dutchman discovered a way of "packing" herring, gutting and salting them so that they could be preserved in barrels and shipped to distant markets, Venice in particular.

Pepper, long imported from the East and an essential ingredient in medieval cooking, continued to be prized. Demand did not begin to level off, and then decline, until the middle of the seventeenth century.

Amid so much continuity there was nevertheless one novelty assured of a fine future: alcohol. Its fortune was slow in being made, however. As Braudel remarks, if the sixteenth century created alcohol, it was the eighteenth that popularized it.[11] Brandy, produced especially in monasteries, was commonly prescribed by physicians and apothecaries as a remedy against plague, gout, and loss of voice. It did not become a festive drink until the sixteenth century. Thereafter its popularity slowly increased, reaching a high point two hundred years later. But kirsch, for example, which came from Alsace, Lorraine, and the Franche-Comté, was still being used in Paris around 1760 for medicinal purposes.

Turning now to the manufacture of metals, an industry in which factory production did not play a role before the technological revolution of the eighteenth century in Great Britain, we note once again a pattern of continuity from the Middle Ages to the Renaissance and beyond. "Medieval civilization in its material aspect," Mathieu Arnoux observes, "was based on iron as much as it was on wood."[12] Iron was employed in rather considerable quantities both in the construction of the cathedrals and in the fabrication of agricultural tools, particularly the plow and moldboard. The growing use of horses, not only as draft animals but also as chargers in combat, led to the increasingly familiar presence in military campaigns of the blacksmith, a figure whose social status rose as a result. Workshops were many and gave employment to workers in a range of related trades: metalworkers, the engineers of their day,[13] who designed and manufactured arms; ironmongers, who reduced iron ore and brought the purified metal to market; also nailsmiths, locksmiths, boilermakers, skilled itinerant workers specializing in the repair of iron objects, and so on.

The appearance of occupational names testifies to the spread of iron. In a large part of Europe, particularly western Europe in the thirteenth century, when patronymics referring to a particular trade first began to come into common use, names of ironworkers multiplied: in France one finds Fèvre, Lefèvre, and so on; in Great Britain, Smith; in the Germanic countries, Schmit in its various spellings. (A personal aside: in the Celtic language of Brittany, Breton, the blacksmith is called "le goff.")

A concern with fashion in clothing is often said to have arisen in the fifteenth and sixteenth centuries, but again we will be able to trace its origin to the heart of the Middle Ages, the thirteenth century, when the first sumptuary laws were decreed by sovereigns and cities. The great German sociologist Norbert Elias, whom I have already mentioned more than once, and whose works have nourished the social sciences since the Second World War, showed that the attempt to formulate standards of civilized behavior goes back to the Middle Ages. In one of his most important works, *Wandlungen der Gesellschaft*,[14] Elias follows the course of the civilizing impulse throughout Europe from the eleventh century until the eighteenth, the moment when the word *progress* was first used in its modern sense. Until then, progress had been perceptible only in the form of intermittent spasms of change or novelty that, following the example of nineteenth-century medievalists, we are now accustomed to call "renaissances." Medieval scholars, fascinated by the idea of Greco-Roman antiquity as a pinnacle of civilization, had supposed that these rebirths would cause society in both its material and cultural aspects eventually to revert to the classical ideal.

The encroachment of civilized behavior in the routines of daily life is of particular interest to Elias, and he makes a careful study of the emergence of table manners in the central Middle Ages, especially the thirteenth century.[15] Anticipating the gradual introduction of the fork in the West, they took the form initially of individual place settings (so that several diners no longer shared a single plate and a single soup bowl) and made it obligatory, for example, for hands to be washed before and after the meal. A still more remarkable change of habit, even if it was never to be completely achieved, came in response to the new prohibition against spitting at the table.

Politeness in a more general sense was another manifestation of the same tendency. Elias sees it as an outgrowth of medieval courtesy. By the seventeenth and eighteenth centuries, having won the favor of the nobility in the first place through their adoption by monarchical and princely courts five hundred years earlier, refined manners had spread among the bourgeoisie and even the lower classes to some extent. In medieval literature the institution of the court was often a subject of satire and disapproval. One thinks in particular of the English king Henry II (1154–89), whose knights were mocked for their effeminacy in Walter Map's pamphlet *De nugis curialium* (Courtiers' Trifles, late twelfth century). Over time, however, the court came to acquire an air of prestige, so that it was looked up to, nowhere more than in France before the Revolution, as a model of proper conduct.

From the political point of view, in an age marked by private wars among feudal lords, there was a pacifying tendency as well. Nathalie Heinich has argued that, beginning with the Peace and Truce of God movement in the eleventh century, unrestrained violence steadily subsided until the middle of the eighteenth century. During this period the West was able not only to enjoy growing prosperity but also the fruits of civilization. "The dynamic of this movement," Heinich says, summarizing Elias's thesis, "arose from the formation of the state, thanks to the gradual establishment of a dual royal monopoly: a monopoly on taxation, which monetarized relations between sovereign and nobles; and a monopoly on legitimate violence, which placed military force in the hands of the king alone—the condition of any [attempts at] pacification."[16] In the meantime the economy remained essentially agrarian, and peasants long continued to be creatures of their lords.

The medieval landscape in Europe was covered with cathedrals. Improvements in artillery, as I indicated earlier, caused fortified castles to be turned into palatial residences, of which Chambord was the most dazzling and Versailles the most prestigious. Pictorial representation developed with the invention in Flanders of easel painting, and the portrait, which appeared at the beginning of the fourteenth century, became one of the nobility's most treasured possessions. With the advent of the Reformation, Christendom was plunged into discord and violence. Yet in spite of the unprecedented intensity of religious strife, Christianity remained the faith of most people, either in its Catholic or Protestant form, until the mid-eighteenth century.

The form of government was stable on the whole as well. Although the United Provinces were created as a republic in 1579, and although unrest in England led to the fall and death of King Charles I in 1649, the monarchy remained dominant in the West until the French Revolution.

In the interval advances in learning had been both steady and gradual, so that by the mid-eighteenth century a group of French intellectuals felt the need to assemble the products of this long and patient accumulation of knowledge in a unified work. Under the editorship of Diderot and d'Alembert, the twenty-eight volumes of the *Encyclopédie* published between 1751 and 1772 marked the end of one period and the beginning of another.

Geopolitical balance in Europe seemed to have been restored at last with the treaties of Utrecht (1713–15), which put an end to the War of the Spanish Succession and to upheaval in most of the continent. The last great traditional conflict is generally considered to have been the War of the Austrian Succession (1740–48), a struggle involving most of the European powers and culminating in the victory of the French over the English and the Dutch at Fontenoy.

1492. A glorious year? I have already said that it was indisputably a decisive moment. But its influence on the course of history can be interpreted in different ways, which is why Christopher Columbus's discovery that year of what was soon to be called America presents the historian with a fascinating case to ponder in relation to the problem of periodization.

The problems this famous date poses have been examined by a great many authors concerned with the Middle Ages and the Renaissance. From an abundant literature I shall briefly consider two books, each by a distinguished historian. The first, Franco Cardini's *Europa 1492*, appeared in 1989;[17] the second, Bernard Vincent's *1492: L'année admirable*, came out two years later.[18]

In the late fifteenth century, Cardini observes, the name *Europe* was commonly used to refer to a political reality. He discusses the relationship of mutual dependence that obtained between the countryside, on the one hand, predominant in respect of both population and area, and towns and cities, on the other, which not only provided consumers of raw materials, particularly food-stuffs, but also a measure of economic protection in years when harvests were poor. The nobility lived luxuriously in its newly demilitarized manor houses, both in town and country. Social classes intermingled—in the public squares of cities in the center and south of Europe, in their grand churches and guildhalls, and on the roads leading north. On festive occasions everyone danced, the nobles in their mansions, the lower classes in the streets. Bath houses, which supplied both hot water and opportunities for sexual pleasure, competed with the churches where people went to pray.

With regard to technology, Europe in the fifteenth century was a playground for inventors. The same thing can be said for painters exploiting new techniques of perspective in painting. Cardini stresses the exceptional role played by Italy as an incubator of innovation and creativity, which extended even to political life with the formation of independent communal regimes in the northern and central regions.

The fifteenth century nevertheless did have another, much darker face. Suffering and hardship were often extreme. Christendom was sorely afflicted by three evils: plague, hunger, and war. This was the age of *danses macabres* and a grim obsession with the "arts of dying." But Cardini detects signs of vitality as well, especially the lure of overseas commerce, which since the early Middle Ages had chiefly been concentrated on the spice trade. Dreams of wealth inspired the exploration of the African coasts and, later, the search for an ocean route to the East Indies that finally led Columbus to set sail in 1492. Although many on Columbus's caravels, and elsewhere in the world from which he came, hoped to discover gold, the Genoese navigator himself was motivated primarily by a desire to lead the pagans toward the true God, the God of the Christians. Columbus was very much a man of the Middle Ages.

Ultimately what Cardini sees at the end of the year 1492, in rendering what he calls an "homage to the Admiral," is the passing of an era: "The Middle Ages ended, the modern age dawned, and the world became suddenly larger."[19] Even though he makes the Middle Ages die at that moment, Cardini insists on continuity, that is, a broadening of perspectives in a time that otherwise remained unchanged. He speaks not of a "Renaissance" but of a "world"— the medieval world that produced Christopher Columbus.

The question for the historian, then, becomes this: in the enlargement brought about in 1492, which is more important, that which ends or that which continues?

Bernard Vincent likewise sees 1492 as a summary of the Christian past and an announcement of Christian glory yet to come—hence his book's subtitle. Vincent begins by deploring the tendency to reduce this year to Columbus's discovery. He then goes on to work out the implications of four exceptional events that occurred that year, each of which, he maintains, disrupted historical continuity. Starting with the Iberian Peninsula, he examines first the surrender of the Muslim sultan of Granada, the last city in Christendom held by Islam. Next he considers the expulsion of the Jews from Spain. The same thing had occurred in England and France two hundred years earlier, of course, but the Catholic kings of Spain long hesitated, hoping apparently that more concerted efforts at conversion would make expulsion unnecessary. As it turned out, the year 1492 can be regarded as glorious only from the point of view of their Christian subjects, who saw Christendom's two great enemies, Islam and Judaism, driven from the country almost simultaneously.

The third event Vincent recalls issued from a resolute determination in the Christian West to create national states. In Spain, 1492 ushered in the use of a single language, Castilian, throughout the land. Antonio de Nebrija (1444–1522), the celebrated grammarian from Andalusia who is usually called a humanist out of respect for the spirit of the age in which he lived, but who in fact had been trained in theology at Salamanca and Bologna before entering the service of the archbishop of Seville, presented Isabella the Catholic with a printed copy of the Castilian grammar he had just published on 18 August 1492. The event was marked by a modest ceremony that concealed its immense and unsuspected significance. On that occasion Nebrija might well have adopted as his own the words of an Aragonese contemporary who was translating the *Historia monachorum in Aegypto* (Lives of the Desert Fathers) into Castilian, words that superbly express the link between language and politics: "Since royal power today is Castilian, and because the excellent kings and queens who govern us have chosen to make the kingdom of Castile the base and the seat of their states, I have decided to write this book in Castilian, for the language, more than any other, accompanies power."[20]

Vincent is surely right to single out the linguistic element from among the various things that structure history into periods: Europe was poised to become a Europe of nations and of languages.[21] And whether or not 1492 was in fact a glorious year, the reasons for its influence go well beyond the discovery that October of the island of Guanahani in the archipelago of the Bahamas, renamed San Salvador by Columbus—the last of Vincent's four events. Even so, must we really consider it Year One of a new period in history?

The British literary historian Helen Cooper has recently argued that William Shakespeare (1564–1616) was a man and a writer of the Middle Ages, not the Renaissance. "The world in which Shakespeare lived was a medieval one," she points out. "Stratford and its surrounding towns had been founded in the Middle Ages:

Coventry, which owed its status as a city to its Norman cathedral; Warwick, grown up around its castle; Oxford, fortified with castle and walls early in the Middle Ages, and given fame by the development of its university in the late twelfth century."[22]

When Shakespeare came to London, sometime between 1585 and 1590, its towers and churches were no longer dominated by the high steeple of the Gothic cathedral of Saint Paul, destroyed by lightning in 1561. Entry to the walled city was through one of the great gates overlooked by a "palace-fortress," the Tower of London, with its old keep, the massive White Tower, built by William the Conqueror but now popularly attributed to Julius Caesar.[23]

From the antiquarian John Stow's *Survey of London* (1598) we know that there were still many abbeys and convents devoted to contemplation and that country lanes meandered through farmland within the city walls. The games played in the streets resembled ones of the twelfth and thirteenth centuries. Most schools and markets had been founded in the Middle Ages. Stow's London was a place filled with nostalgia for bygone days, and Shakespeare could hardly have been untouched by it. Printing, a recent invention, helped the works of Geoffrey Chaucer (c. 1340–1400), ballads such as the one of Robin Hood, and epic poems about medieval heroes to reach a broader and predominantly lay readership. The first book printed in English was the *Morte Darthur* by Sir Thomas Mallory in 1485.[24]

Shakespeare seems to have wished at the beginning of his career to become a fashionable poet, imitating the literary models of antiquity, but he rapidly immersed himself in the life of the theater. Breaking with the conventions of classical Greek drama, he conceived of the playhouse as "an encyclopedia of the world, *theatrum mundi*."[25] And on the stage of this world in miniature, his first interest was to recount tales of the English Middle Ages.

For inspiration Shakespeare looked to medieval authors. He often resorted to allegory, and three types of character occupy a central place in his plays: king, shepherd, and fool. Fantastic beings frequently intervene, fairies in *A Midsummer Night's Dream*, for example, and sprites such as Ariel in *The Tempest*. The theme of the danse macabre, in which medieval attitudes toward death receive their fullest expression, is developed in *Cymbeline*.[26] In a concluding chapter Cooper sees Shakespeare as a new Chaucer, an artist who adapted the Middle Ages of the great English poet of the fourteenth century for the stage while using similar metrical devices.

In 2011 the American science journalist Charles C. Mann published a book called *1493* that enjoyed considerable success in the United States. Its subtitle, *Uncovering the New World Columbus Created*, may seem to suggest that it is a work of history. It is nothing of the sort. It is a dream, a fantasy. It purports to describe what the world became when Columbus returned home, in March 1493, bringing back with him, from what he did not yet believe to be a new continent, "golden ornaments, brilliantly colored parrots, and as many as ten captive Indians."[27] Introducing a neologism, Mann says that Columbus's voyages "marked the beginning of a new biological era: the Homogenocene"—that is, an era characterized by "homogenizing, mixing unlike substances to create a uniform blend."[28] This, he maintains, is the condition to which the phenomenon known as globalization ultimately tends. The term *homogenocene* may possibly be of some use in describing certain patterns of convergence in exchange and communication, but it corresponds to no intrinsic property of either geophysical or human evolution that I am aware of. Most cultural geographers today are still primarily concerned, it seems to me, with the diversity of regions and peoples.

Mann waxes poetic about maritime exploration and commerce. He sings of transatlantic voyages, with tobacco on one side of the sea, evil air[29] on the other, and of transpacific voyages, with silver on one side and rice on the other. Europe is analyzed as an exporter of agricultural and industrial products, on the one hand, and as an importer of oil—but here we are far from the Middle Ages and the Renaissance! As for Africa, the discovery of America is seen as amounting to the birth of a new world as well, condemned as it was for several centuries to furnish the slaves necessary for the continent's economic development. By way of conclusion Mann imagines that he has been able to pinpoint the place where the dream of globalization was finally realized, in the Philippines. There, he says, Asia, Europe, and America met for the first time.[30] For now, at least, the dream has come to an end.

Before coming to what I believe to be the end of a long Middle Ages, around the middle of the eighteenth century, and before saying how the problem of the periodization of history looks to me in the light of everything that has been said so far, I should like to illustrate by means of one further example the continuity that, to my way of thinking, indisputably characterizes the relationship between the Middle Ages and the Renaissance: the genesis of the modern state. For more than a thousand years, beginning in the seventh century, the West followed a long and, in the main, unbroken course of development. Nowhere was this stability more remarkable than in the sphere of government. To be sure, momentary disruptions did occur prior to the French Revolution, but they had little lasting effect. One thinks of England, for example, where political life was gravely disturbed in the seventeenth century with the beheading of Charles I and the abdication of James II, but the monarchy survived. The only significant novelty was the independence of the United Provinces, achieved by means of a treaty signed in 1579 and confirmed in 1609, the Union of Utrecht, which established the first Western republic.

The discovery of America, and the extraction of abundant quantities of two precious metals in particular, gold and silver, stimulated the formation of a monetary economy in Europe, but it did not immediately give rise to capitalism. The creation of the modern state was a slow process: the monarchy claimed new powers for itself only gradually, with the result that the distinctive institutions of centralized government were devised in a piecemeal manner.[31] Jean-Philippe Genet makes an incisive point in this connection:

> In the twelfth century a new and autonomous field came into being, law. Little by little, other fields achieved their own independence: literature, which presupposed a sufficiently

large audience of people who could read, followed by medicine and, later, the natural sciences and politics. In other words, the emergence of the state was accompanied by a gradual fragmentation of the predominant field of theology, itself a consequence of the secularization of a society in which advanced cultural tools were more and more widely available. And if one examines the constitution and development of these fields, at every level one finds the state.[32]

The British historian Michael Clanchy has likewise insisted on the long apprenticeship required in order to learn to write,[33] a skill that at the turn of the sixteenth century began to be acquired by women.

With regard to law and politics, Jacques Krynen emphasizes the importance of treatises composed around 1300 and the fact that much of the vocabulary of medieval canon law—terms such as *auctoritas*, *utilitas publica*, *privilegium*—prefigures the terminology of modern administrative law.[34] Michel Pastoureau, for his part, recalls the history of the royal seal, a potent symbol of the state in both medieval and early modern Europe.[35] In the domain of public administration the finest pictorial allegory is to be found in the heart of the Middle Ages: the memorable scenes that make up part of the famous cycle of frescoes by Ambrogio Lorenzetti in the Palazzo Pubblico of Siena, *The Allegory of Good Government* and *The Effects of Good Government* (1337–38).[36]

Following a brief period of favor in the ninth century, the lily (*lys*) became in the twelfth century, through the efforts of Abbot

Suger, the symbol of the French monarchy in the necropolis of the Capetian kings, the abbey church of Saint-Denis. As Jean-Louis Biget, Jean-Claude Hervé, and Yvon Thébert have shown, however, it was not until 1400 or so, shortly after *Le roman de la fleur de lys* was composed, that the legend of the lily's heavenly origin was given its final form—another potent symbol whose influence was to be felt until the French Revolution.[37]

The intensity of popular devotion to the Virgin, from the late eleventh century onward, is also well known. It was the twelfth century that marked the appearance of the Coronation of the Virgin, an iconographic theme that likewise was to live on as long as the medieval monarchy survived.

It is not surprising that the first sponsors of the idea of the Renaissance as a period in its own right should have been mightily impressed by the Age of Discovery. The voyages of exploration undertaken during this era did give an enduring impetus to trade; there can be no doubt of that. I have already remarked on the consequences of the expansion of maritime commerce to the Indian Ocean, the coasts of Africa, and, above all, the Americas. It needs to be kept in mind, however, that the introduction of foods and beverages that had previously been unknown in the Old World (the tomato, of course, as well as tea and, later and more tentatively, coffee) did not profoundly modify the diet of Europeans, which continued to be based on cereals, bread, gruel, and meat. An important event, although it seems to me a less decisive one than the advent of regular commercial service between Italian ports and those of northern Europe in the late thirteenth century, was the founding of the Dutch companies (in 1602) and French companies (by Colbert in 1664 and later by Law in 1719) that developed and concentrated international trade in commodities.

Finance is often considered, along with culture, to be a leading indicator of the West's emergence from the Middle Ages. And yet Carlo M. Cipolla, in a classic work of lively and meticulous scholarship, showed that prior to the industrial revolution of the eighteenth century there was only one real economy, based on agriculture. What is more, although "the levels of productivity prevailing in Europe at the end of the sixteenth century were considerably higher than they had been six hundred years earlier, . . . they were still abysmally low."[38]

Nevertheless a primitive monetary economy did begin to take shape in the aftermath of the discovery of America, to such a degree, in fact, that one can speak of progress in the seventeenth century. The abundance of precious metals, combined with the diffusion and growing complexity of banking techniques having their origin in the Middle Ages, led to the slow but inexorable rise of capitalism. In the absence of this secular tendency the first stock market, conventionally dated to the creation of the Bank of Amsterdam in 1609, could have had no reason to come into existence. And yet one cannot reasonably speak of "capitalism" at this particular moment; indeed, prior to the late eighteenth century and the publication of the great work by the Scottish economist Adam Smith, *An Inquiry Into the Nature and Causes of the Wealth of Nations* (1776), economic life cannot be said to have outgrown the scale it knew during the Middle Ages or to have changed in any other fundamental way.

The proponents of the Renaissance as a period also treat the Reformation as a major turning point, marking the end of the monopoly enjoyed by the Roman Church, until then the sole target of heretical dissent. Yet not even the horrors of the wars of religion in the sixteenth century could undermine the Christian faith of people in the West, which remained effectively complete until the eighteenth century.

Nevertheless religious observance gradually declined, and the weakening of belief that accompanied it was to have profound consequences for philosophy and literature. A more or less irreligious spirit of rationalism grew up in England under the influence of Thomas Hobbes (1588–1679) and John Locke (1632–1704), and even more so in France on account of the work of Pierre Bayle (1647–1706), author of a four-volume *Dictionnaire historique et critique* that appeared between 1695 and 1697. Bayle had settled in Rotterdam, where he could teach without interference by the authorities, the new Dutch Republic having guaranteed all who resided there freedom of conscience and expression—a sign that the Middle Ages was on the verge of entering a new era. The actual emergence of this era as the successor to a long Middle Ages that extended beyond the Renaissance was signaled, in my view, by the publication in 1751 of the *Encyclopédie ou dictionnaire raisonné des sciences, des arts et des métiers*, which, owing to the heroic exertions not only of Diderot and D'Alembert but also of Voltaire, Montesquieu,

Rousseau, and other contributors, affirmed the preeminence of reason and science over Christian dogma.

Like a seal set on the state of mind of a society that was at last breaking with the Middle Ages and becoming truly modern, the word *progress* was employed (probably for the first time in 1757) to mean the "forward movement of civilization toward an ever more flourishing condition."[39] The new way of thinking that was being formed in the West, and that was born with the French Revolution, marked the triumph of progress and something more as well: the triumph of the individual.

By way of conclusion, in a short final chapter, I shall try to set forth a general justification for dividing history into periods, already illustrated at some length by my pleading on behalf of a long Middle Ages as a particular case. First, however, allow me to recapitulate. Without going into unnecessary detail, it is enough simply to say that the first centuries of the Christian era marked the passage from a period that was not to be called "antiquity" until 1580 (in the first edition of Montaigne's *Essays*) and that was meant to refer only to ancient Greece and Rome.

The periodization elaborated by classical authors and subsequently adopted by Saint Augustine, who then bequeathed it to the Middle Ages, provided for six ages, modeled on the six ages of life. It introduced the idea of the aging of the world, which by Augustine's time had reached its sixth and last phase.

Dread of the approaching end was to be almost constantly combated during the early and central Middle Ages by another idea, the notion of rebirth (*renovatio*). So fervently was it embraced at certain points that modern historians have identified several "renaissances": the Carolingian renaissance of the eighth and ninth centuries, to begin with, but even more strikingly the renaissance of the twelfth century, which in both economic life (improved farming techniques) and intellectual life (School of Saint Victor, the teachings of Abelard, and the *Sentences* of Peter Lombard [1100–1160], used as a textbook in the new universities) was an era of growth and innovation. The Middle Ages, thought to be senescent, were nevertheless constantly alert to novelty—a harbinger of the idea of progress, though, as I say, this name was not to be applied until much later. One thinks of the repeated use of the term *novus* (new) in the life of Saint Francis of Assisi composed by his earliest biographer, Thomas of Celano, in the thirteenth century.

The era extending from the twelfth century to the fifteenth was one of slow but steady technological development. In agriculture its emblems were the iron plowshare, the replacement of oxen by draft horses, and the increased yields made possible by triennial crop rotation; in what was later to be called industry, the operation of mills on a larger scale than before, together with inventions such as the hydraulic saw and, from the end of the twelfth century, the windmill. In religion and intellectual life, change took the form of the Church's affirmation of the sacraments, the founding of universities, and the rise of scholasticism.

These innovations came about at a time when, particularly in literature and philosophy, there was a turning back to what were now considered to be the unsurpassable virtues of Greco-Roman antiquity. This is why modern historians were to give it an upper-cased name, the Renaissance. In the central Middle Ages people had had the sense of going forward while looking back over their shoulder. For a long time this perception prevented them from seeing that a new periodization was possible.

The situation changed in the fourteenth century, when Petrarch cast the preceding millennium into darkness by demeaning it as a neutral and dull period of transition between the splendor of antiquity and the time of renewal that he announced. He gave these intermediate centuries the name *media aetas*—and so the Middle Age was born (or Middle Ages, as they were to be known in English). The period that many scholars and artists in the fifteenth and sixteenth centuries thought they were bringing into existence did not receive its own name until 1840, from Michelet during his first lecture that year at the Collège de France. But the ground for a new periodization (restricted to the history of the Western world, it must be emphasized) had been prepared long before by the evolution of history itself: once a literary genre, it was now a subject of formal instruction. The transfer of history from the realm of entertainment to the domain of learning had been accomplished for the most part in schools and universities. Following the example of Germany, where, as we saw, history was first recognized as an independent branch of knowledge, chairs of history were established initially at the university level in a number of countries, and then, beginning in the late eighteenth and early nineteenth centuries, history was taught as a required subject in schools. By 1820 the metamorphosis was complete in much of Europe.

The proponents of the Renaissance as a specific period consider a certain number of events that occurred in the fifteenth and sixteenth centuries to have been decisive. The most impressive of these is perhaps the discovery of America by Christopher Columbus in 1492. But others were scarcely less important over the long term: in religion, the replacement of a unified Christian faith by the division of Europeans into two denominations, reformed Christianity and its traditional version, now known as Catholicism; in politics, the strengthening of the powers of the absolute monarchy for the purpose of governing newly created nation-states (with the notable exception of the republican United Provinces, founded in 1579); in philosophy and literature, the growing appeal of libertinism and secularism; in economics and finance, the dramatic expansion of the money supply, a result of suddenly abundant reserves of precious metals, and the development of the capitalist system, accelerated by the founding in 1609 of the Bank of Amsterdam.

My own view is that the transition from one period to another, in this case at the end of a long Middle Ages, is to be situated in the mid-eighteenth century. It coincides with the implementation of agricultural reforms first advocated in France by the Physiocrats; the invention of the steam engine, conceived by the French physicist Denis Papin (1647–1712) and realized by the Scottish engineer

James Watt (1736–1819) in 1769; and the birth of modern industry, which spread from Great Britain throughout the Continent. In philosophy and religion the long Middle Ages came to a close at last with the work that introduced rational and secular thought as well as modern science and technology, the *Encyclopédie*, of which Voltaire and Diderot were the leading lights. In politics the end of the medieval period corresponds to the rise of the antimonarchical movement that culminated in the French Revolution.

The Australian historian David Garrioch has studied how this movement developed over the course of the eighteenth century.[40] In Paris alone "society changed in every respect: the appearance of new social, economic, and demographic behaviors left no one untouched, pulling ancient communities apart, undermining traditional attachments to fraternal orders, religious orders, professions, guilds, customary practices of every sort; and giving rise to novel forms of social cohesion, to profound religious, political, and institutional changes."[41]

If we add to all of these things the widening gap between rich and poor (a sign of economic and financial transformation), the growing taste for reading and the theater, among other pleasures, and the deepening concern with individual success, it becomes clear that it was not until the middle of the eighteenth century that the West may truly be said to have entered a new period.

In closing, let me restate the argument by looking once more at the relationship between the Middle Ages and the Renaissance, this time in a way that will make it easier, or so I hope, to see what a historical period really amounts to.

For this purpose I refer to a special issue of the popular science magazine *Les Cahiers de science & vie* that appeared recently under the title "The Genius of the Renaissance: When Europe Reinvented Itself."[42] Following a brief discussion of what they call the "spirit" of the Renaissance, the editors survey various opinions regarding the return to ancient sources signified by the name of the new age, place Florence at its center, and praise the "awakening of reason" that it brought about.

In all these respects, however, surely the Renaissance did no more than prolong the Middle Ages. The Middle Ages themselves grew directly out of antiquity, and, if not all of medieval theology, then at least scholasticism from the twelfth century onward relied habitually on rationalist argumentation. As for locating the emergence of a new period in Florence, this, it seems to me, amounts to an inexact sort of historical reductionism that has the effect of making the Renaissance the invention of a small group of politicians and artists.

The editors also identify the Renaissance with a way of "reconceiving" humanity. And yet this decisive change in orientation, which meant that theology could no longer be contemplated apart from humanism, occurred during the Middle Ages. The renaissance of the twelfth century insisted that man was made "in the image of God"—an idea that was echoed by all the great scholastics of the following century, Saint Thomas not least among them, who proclaimed that the true subject of their philosophy, apprehended through God, was man. Humanism itself had a long history whose medieval roots can be traced back to antiquity.

The editors go on to associate the Renaissance with the "birth of scientific method." Here they have three things uppermost in mind: rational inquiry, the primacy of mathematics, and a growing interest in controlled, systematic experimentation. I have already talked at some length about the question of rationality. With regard to mathematics it needs to be borne in mind that its emergence as a practical instrument of calculation occurred in the Middle Ages with the appearance of new and more accurate editions of Euclid, accompanied by commentaries on his geometry; with the adoption of so-called Arabic numerals (including zero), largely under the influence of Leonardo of Pisa's landmark book on arithmetic, the *Liber abaci*, composed in 1202 and revised in 1228; also with technical innovations in trade and banking (among them the bill of exchange, introduced at the beginning of the fourteenth century). What was in fact new, but is properly seen as part of a medieval renaissance of the fifteenth and sixteenth centuries, was the interest in careful physical experiments and, in medicine, particularly in the sixteenth century, autopsy.

The editors of this issue of *Les Cahiers de science & vie* are also very much mistaken, in my view, in asserting that pluralism emerged in Europe only in the sixteenth century. Since the early Middle Ages, Christendom had constantly been torn by disputes over what the Church called "heresies," many of them brought before ecclesiastical tribunals. Today, of course, we find it difficult not to regard these offenses against orthodoxy as so many novel theories and conjectures—original ways of thinking whose variance with accepted teaching would better have been welcomed than punished. Diversity of many kinds was both lively and widespread in the Middle Ages. One finds evidence of it even in food and cooking (although the Danish author of the oldest medieval cookbook, from the early twelfth century, had studied in Paris and fallen under the spell of French cuisine, already in its ascendancy).

Another characteristic feature of the Renaissance, according to the editors, is the powerful "inspiration" it carried abroad from Italy. This may be less objectionable than trying to identify the new period with the activity of a few exceptionally talented people in Florence. Ever since the early Middle Ages, the originality—indeed, the precocity—of Italy, whether in respect of the papacy, the communes, or the principalities, had been a constant condition of Christian Europe. And yet the roles played by what are sometimes called the German Renaissance and the French Renaissance (limited for the most part in the latter case, however, to the châteaus of the Loire) were not therefore insignificant or unoriginal in their own way, as I have tried to indicate.

The reality is that in the course of the Middle Ages there were a number of renaissances, more or less extensive, more or less triumphant. As for the construction of magnificent country seats, this novelty goes back to the medieval period, as we have seen, with the transformation of fortified castles into palatial residences, opening onto the world rather than closed in on themselves, from the early fourteenth century onward. A similar transition may be observed in clothing, where the long robe or gown of the early

Middle Ages gave way to the doublet of the *ancien régime*. The doublet disappeared once and for all only with changes in the styles of middle- and working-class dress in the nineteenth century.

What might be called Middle Ages–Renaissance continuity and Long Middle Ages–Modern Times discontinuity perhaps most clearly manifest themselves with regard to industrial production. It is true that blast furnaces, for example, became progressively larger during the Renaissance. But it was not until the power of the steam engine began to be harnessed that industry in the modern sense came into existence in Great Britain, from there spreading throughout the Continent. And although exceptional importance is rightly attached to printing, which as everyone knows was invented in the mid-fifteenth century, still more fundamental revolutions, in literacy and reading habits, had taken place earlier. With the dawning of the Middle Ages the roll was superseded by the codex. For almost a thousand years, until the thirteenth century, manuscripts were copied by hand in monastic *scriptoria,* at which point production moved outside the monastery into commercial workshops that came to be affiliated with the new universities. Also in the thirteenth century, in Italy, books began to be made by breaking up a text into more easily reproduced sections known as *peciae* (hence the so-called pecia system of manufacture). Finally, the use of paper (rather than parchment) spread from Spain beginning in the twelfth century and then, to an even greater degree, from Italy in the early thirteenth.

We have seen, too, that no theory of capitalism was developed, nor indeed did capitalism even become aware of its own existence, until the publication of Adam Smith's great work in 1776. In the meantime the discoveries that followed the early voyages of Columbus and Vasco de Gama did not succeed in stimulating commerce on a scale large enough to sustain European colonization before the conquest of India by Great Britain in 1756. With regard to navigation, as I say, the essential advances had already occurred in the early thirteenth century with the adoption of the compass and the sternpost rudder.

Finally, the editors of this special issue of *Les Cahiers de science & vie* credit the Renaissance with inventing the idea of progress. This seems to me unfortunate. Although it is in fact possible to show, contrary to the opinion of earlier historians, that the Middle Ages had a quite developed awareness of novelty and improvement,[43] the modern meaning of *progress* emerged only in the eighteenth century. The crucial fact, I believe, is that the conventionally uppercased Renaissance of the fifteenth and sixteenth centuries—what I consider instead to be the last of a series of medieval renaissances—was the harbinger of a truly modern age, not the age itself, which did not begin to unfold until about 1750. The manifesto of this modernity, following on more than a thousand years of domination by the Christian religion in both its Catholic and reformed versions, was, as I have said more than once and now repeat again, the *Encyclopédie*. Indeed, to judge from the titles they give the last two sections ("Cosmos: A Revolution *in the Making*" and "The Expeditions of the Sixteenth Century *Herald* the Globalization of Today"), the editors themselves seem to have sensed the long gestation that took place.[44]

Allow me, then, before I conclude this brief essay, to emphasize one basic point: a "true" historical period usually lasts a long time. It is not free of change, of course, because history never stands still. As it evolves, it experiences renaissances, more or less great, more or less brilliant. These rebirths often depend on the past, for they grow out of a certain nostalgic fascination felt by the people of a particular time. But this past is a peculiar sort of inheritance. It is what makes it possible to leave one period behind and leap forward to the next.

| Conclusion

Periodization and Globalization

By now it will be plain that I dissent from the view of most modern historians in seeing the Renaissance, not as a separate period, but only as the last subperiod of a long Middle Ages.

Periodization in the Western tradition goes back to the earliest Greek thinking about history (Herodotus, fifth century BCE) and, still further, to the Hebrew Bible (Daniel, sixth century BCE). Even so, it did not become a matter of broad agreement among historians until quite recently, the eighteenth and the nineteenth centuries, when the writing of history itself underwent a transformation: what had been a purely literary genre was now considered a branch of knowledge worthy of being taught to the young. As a subject of instruction it responded to a desire, as well as a need, to make sense of the great spans of time over which human societies have developed. Calendars made it possible to organize the moments of daily life. Periodization satisfied the same purpose, but over a longer term. The question arises whether this human invention, if it is to have lasting value, has to correspond to some objective reality. It seems to me that it must. In saying this, I do not refer to the world as a physical system. By "reality," I mean human reality—the lives actually lived by people, particularly in the West. The history of these people's lives, so far as we are able to reconstruct them on the basis of the various materials available to us, constitutes a distinguishable chapter of human experience having its own characteristic features. One of these is a distinctive rhythm of events that causes the history of people in the West to coincide with a particular succession of periods.

The act of periodizing is justified by all those things that make history a science—not an exact science, of course, but nevertheless a social science that rests on an objective foundation built up from documentary and other sources. Now, the events that these sources describe unavoidably follow a certain course: as Marc Bloch used to say, the history of societies unfolds over time. Since history, by its very nature, evolves, it is inseparable from time. Historians have no choice but to try to bend chronology to their own will. At the same time, they cannot help but find themselves under its sway. To the extent that the conditions of life undergo change, all the more indispensable does periodization become for the historian.

The idea of a *longue durée*, a term due to Fernand Braudel and widely used by historians since, has been objected to on the ground that it has the effect of blurring periods, if not actually erasing them. To my mind there is no contradiction. Not only is there room for periods in the long term, they are a necessity—for the attempt to explain events that have both a mental and a physical dimension, as historical events inescapably do, requires a combination of continuity and discontinuity. It is just this advantage that the idea of a *longue durée* offers the historian when it is supplemented by the freedom to divide the course of history into periods.

The question of the rate of historical change—or, to put it another way, how quickly one period gives way to another—I have left to one side because it seems not to have really interested anyone until the modern era. People during the Middle Ages and the Renaissance, unlike historians of the recent past and the present day, were more impressed by how *slowly* history changes. There have been few, if any, genuine revolutions. François Furet was fond of saying that the French Revolution lasted for almost the whole of the nineteenth century. This, by the way, is why many historians, including ones who subscribe to the notion of a specific period called the Renaissance, have resorted to the expression "Middle Ages and Renaissance." If one century falls under this head more naturally than any of its neighbors (and for just this reason displays unrivaled richness and creativity), it is surely the fifteenth.

My own view is that we will come nearer to the truth, and with greater hope of thinking about periodization in a way that stands to make the study of history both feasible and rewarding, if we consider that periods are typically long and typically marked by phases of significant, though not epochal, change. In the case of the Middle Ages these subperiods are usefully called *renaissances*, a term that joins a sense of novelty (*naissance*) to the idea of a return to a golden age (the prefix *re-* pointing backward in time while suggesting a resemblance between past and present).

There is another reason to suppose that dividing history into periods is not only possible but necessary. Of the two perspectives that arouse the greatest enthusiasm among historians today, the long term and world history (the latter a consequence of the largely American interest in developing the idea of a global past),[1] neither one seems to me incompatible with periodization; quite the contrary. I repeat: unmeasured and measured time coexist. Periodization, however, can apply only to limited domains, or areas, of human civilization. The task of a world history is to discover the relations among these domains. Periodization and globalization are therefore complementary, not contradictory.

But historians must be careful not to confuse, as they have too often done until now, it seems to me, the idea of globalization with that of standardization (or homogenization, as it is sometimes called). There are two stages in globalization: the first consists in communication, the coming into direct contact of regions and civilizations that previously were unfamiliar with one another; the second is a phenomenon of absorption, a fusing of cultures. Until now humanity has passed through only the first of these stages.

Periodization presents historians today with splendid opportunities for fresh research and analysis. Thanks to periodization, both the manner in which human history is organized and the manner in which it changes over time, over the long term, is becoming clearer.

NOTES

PREFACE

1. See in particular the various interviews and articles I published in the journal *L'Histoire*, beginning in 1980, and later collected under the title *Un long Moyen Âge* (Paris: Tallandier, 2004). This book was subsequently brought out in a less expensive paperback edition by Hachette, as part of its Pluriel series, in 2010. [An early summary statement of the present book's argument, "Pour un long Moyen Âge," *Europe*, no. 654 (October 1983), 19–24, was reprinted in the author's 1985 book with Gallimard, available in English as *The Medieval Imagination*, trans. Arthur Goldhammer (Chicago: University of Chicago Press, 1988), 18–23.—Trans.]

2. The rather extensive bibliography at the end is meant to encourage readers to explore more fully questions that, in many cases, I have scarcely touched upon in the text.

PRELUDE: PERIODIZATION AND THE PAST

1. See, for example, Olivier Dumoulin and Raphaël Valéry, eds., *Périodes: La construction du temps historique* (Paris: Éditions de l'EHESS, 1991); also Jean Leduc, "Période, périodisation," in Christian Delacroix, François Dosse, Patrick Garcia, and Nicolas Offenstadt, eds., *Historiographies: Concepts et débats*, 2 vols. (Paris: Gallimard, 2010), 2:830–38. On the notion of an "age" see Auguste Luneau, *L'histoire du salut chez les Pères de l'Église: La doctrine des âges du monde* (Paris: Beauchesne, 1964). Krzysztof Pomian uses the term *epoch* in his great work *L'ordre du temps* (Paris: Gallimard, 1984); see especially the third chapter, "Époques," pages 101–63.

2. See Bernard Guenée, "Histoire," in Jacques Le Goff and Jean-Claude Schmitt, eds., *Dictionnaire raisonné de l'Occident médiéval* (Paris: Fayard, 1999), 483–96.

1. EARLY PERIODIZATIONS

1. Patrick Boucheron, ed., *Histoire du monde au XVᵉ siècle* (Paris: Fayard, 2009).

2. See the table in Philippe Norel, *L'histoire économique globale* (Paris: Seuil, 2009), 243–46.

3. See Agostino Paravicini Bagliani, "Âges de vie," in Le Goff and Schmitt, *Dictionnaire raisonné de l'Occident médiéval*, 7–19.

4. See Daniel 7:13–28.

5. See Pomian, *L'ordre du temps*, 107.

6. In addition to the creators of periods, on the one hand, and of calendars, on the other, there were scholars (known in the medieval world as chronographers) who measured spans of elapsed time. See the excel-

lent account by François Hartog, "Ordre des temps: Chronographie, chronologie, histoire," in Pierre Gibert and Christoph Théobald, eds., *Théologies et vérité au défi de l'histoire* (Leuven: Peeters, 2010), 279–89.

7. Daniel 7:13.

8. See Jacques Le Goff, *À la recherche du temps sacré: Jacques de Voragine et la Légende dorée* (Paris: Perrin, 2011). [An English version appeared shortly before the author's death, under the title *In Search of Sacred Time: Jacobus de Voragine and the Golden Legend*, trans. Lydia G. Cochrane (Princeton, N.J.: Princeton University Press, 2014). Trans.]

9. See John 21:11.

10. Voltaire, *The Age of Louis XIV*, trans. William H. Fleming, in *The Works of Voltaire*, 21 vols. (New York: E. R. DuMont, 1901), 12:5. See also the discussion of this passage in Pomian, *L'ordre du temps*, 123–25.

11. Voltaire, *The Age of Louis XIV*, 6.

12. Ibid., 7.

2. THE LATE APPEARANCE OF THE MIDDLE AGES

1. A close variant of the expression *media aetas* is encountered as early as 1518, in the work of the Swiss scholar Joachim von Watt (Vadianus), and later in 1604, with the German jurist Melchior Goldast von Haiminsfelt, in the form *medium aetum*. See George L. Burr, "How the Middle Ages Got Their Name," *American Historical Review* 20, no. 4 (1915): 838–40. I am grateful to Jean-Claude Schmitt for bringing this article to my attention.

2. Victor Cousin, *Cours de l'histoire de la philosophie*, in *Œuvres*, 3 vols. (Brussels: Hauman, 1840–41), 1:17.

3. See Charles H. Haskins, *The Renaissance of the Twelfth Century* (Cambridge, Mass.: Harvard University Press, 1927).

4. An allusion to the title of Georges Duby's 1976 book, *Le temps des cathédrales*.—Trans.

5. See Eugenio Garin, "Medio Evo e tempi bui: Concetto e polemiche nella storia del pensiero dal XV al XVIII secolo," in Vittore Branca, ed., *Concetto, storia, miti e immagini del Medio Evo* (Florence: Sansoni, 1973), 199–224.

6. See Bertrand Lançon's illuminating study, *L'Antiquité tardive* (Paris: Presses Universitaires de France, 1997).

7. See Ernst Werner, "De l'esclavage à la féodalité: La périodisation de l'histoire mondiale," *Annales ESC* 17, no. 5 (1962): 930–39.

8. See in particular Georges Duby, *L'histoire continue* (Paris: Odile Jacob, 1991); available in English as *History Continues*, trans. Arthur Goldhammer (Chicago: University of Chicago Press, 1994).

3. HISTORY, EDUCATION, PERIODIZATION

1. See Jean-Claude Schmitt, "L'imaginaire du temps dans l'histoire chrétienne," in *Pris-Ma* 25, no. 49–50 (2009): 135–59.

2. See, in particular, François Hartog, *Le miroir d'Hérodote: Essai sur la représentation de l'autre* (Paris: Gallimard, 1980). The many points of contact between myth and epic, on the one hand, and history, on the other, were forged through the development by ancient Greek thinkers, from Homer to Herodotus, of the concept of time. See also François Hartog, ed., *L'histoire d'Homère à Augustin*, trans. Michel Casevitz (Paris: Seuil, 1999).

3. Here I follow the argument developed by Pierre Gibert, with reference to the book of Joshua, in *La Bible à la naissance de l'histoire: Au temps de Saül, David et Salomon* (Paris: Fayard, 1979).

4. See Guenée's edited volume, *Études sur l'historiographie médiévale* (Paris: Publications de la Sorbonne, 1977); also his own later work, *Histoire et culture historique dans l'Occident médiéval* (Paris: Aubier-Montaigne, 1980).

5. See Arnaldo D. Momigliano, "Ancient History and the Antiquarian," *Journal of the Warburg and Courtauld Institutes* 13 (1950): 285–315; repr. in *Studies in Historiography* (London: Weidenfeld and Nicolson, 1966), 1–39.

6. See François de Dainville, *L'éducation des jésuites (XVIe–XVIIIe siècle)* (Paris: Minuit, 1978).

7. See Annie Bruter, *L'histoire enseignée au Grand Siècle: Naissance d'une pédagogie* (Paris: Belin, 1998).

8. As Jean-Claude Dhotel remarked, "Fleury's undertaking, even if it was warmly approved, must not be misinterpreted. In the author's own mind, historical catechism was only a prelude to dogmatic catechism." See Jean-Claude Dhotel, *Les origines du catéchisme moderne d'après les premiers manuels imprimés en France* (Paris: Aubier-Montaigne, 1967), 431.

9. Le Goff seems to be thinking here of Gauchet's discussion in "Les lettres sur l'histoire de France d'Augustin Thierry," in Pierre Nora, ed., *Les lieux de mémoire*, 3 vols. in 7 (Paris: Gallimard, 1984–92), vol. 2: *La nation*, part 1, 247–316.—Trans.

10. Here I have relied especially on the fine essay by Patrick Garcia and Jean Leduc, "Enseignement de l'histoire en France," in Christian Delacroix, François Dosse, Patrick Garcia, and Nicolas Offenstadt, eds., *Historiographies: Concepts et débats*, 2 vols. (Paris: Gallimard, 2010), 1:104–11. [Under Lavisse's direction, what had initially been conceived as a schoolbook grew into a monumental history of France

in twenty-seven volumes, published by Hachette between 1901 and 1923.—Trans.]

11. For the sketch that follows I am indebted chiefly to a remarkable essay by Arnaldo Momigliano, "L'introduzione dell'insegnamento della storia come soggetto accademico e le sue implicazione," in *Tra storia e storicismo* (Pisa: Nistri-Lischi, 1985), 75–96. [This essay first appeared in English as "The Introduction of History as an Academic Subject and Its Implications," *Minerva* 21, no. 1 (1983): 1–15.—Trans.]

12. In addition to the article on history by Bernard Guenée that I cited earlier, see in this connection my own work *Histoire et mémoire* (Paris: Gallimard, 1988); two works by François Hartog, *Croire en l'histoire* (Paris: Flammarion, 2013) and *Évidence de l'histoire: Ce que voient les historiens* (Paris: Éditions de l'EHESS, 2005); also see Reinhart Koselleck, *L'expérience de l'histoire*, ed. Michael Werner, trans. Alexandre Escudier (Paris: Gallimard/Seuil, 1997); and Paul Ricoeur, *La mémoire, l'histoire, l'oubli* (Paris: Seuil, 2000).

4. BIRTH OF THE RENAISSANCE

1. From Michelet's preface to the third edition (1869) of *Histoire de France*, in *Œuvres complètes*, ed. Paul Viallaneix, 21 vols. (Paris: Flammarion, 1971–87), 4:11.

2. See Jacques Le Goff, "Le Moyen Âge de Michelet," in *Pour un autre Moyen Âge: Temps, travail et culture en Occident* (Paris: Gallimard, 1977), 19–45. [Available in English as *Time, Work, and Culture in the Middle Ages*, trans. Arthur Goldhammer (Chicago: University of Chicago Press, 1980).—Trans.]

3. Lucien Febvre, "Comment Jules Michelet inventa la Renaissance," in *Studi in onore di Gino Luzzatto*, 4 vols. (Milan: A. Giuffrè, 1950), 3:1–11.

4. Quoted in ibid., 3:9.
5. Quoted in ibid., 3:11.
6. Jules Michelet, *Cours au Collège de France, 1838–1851*, ed. Paul Viallaneix, 2 vols. (Paris: Gallimard, 1995), 1:339.
7. Ibid., 1:352–53.
8. Ibid., 1:354–55.
9. Ibid., 1:463.
10. Ibid., 1:421–22.
11. Ibid., 1:424.
12. On this point see Girolamo Arnaldi, *L'Italia e i suoi invasori* (Rome: Laterza, 2002).
13. Michelet, *Cours au Collège de France*, 1:434.
14. Ibid., 1:436.
15. Ibid., 1:463.
16. Ibid., 1:464.
17. The publishing history of *The Civilization of the Renaissance in Italy* in its various editions has been reconstructed in a long preface by Robert Kopp to the fine new French edition of Henri Schmitt's translation, revised and corrected by Robert Klein (Paris: Bartillat, 2012), 7–35.
18. See Jacob Burckhardt, *The Civilization of the Renaissance in Italy*, trans S. G. C. Middlemore (New York: Harper and Row, 1958), 21–142.
19. Ibid., 94, 95.
20. Ibid., 107, 113.
21. Thus the title of part 1, chapter 9: see ibid., 115–19.
22. Ibid., 136.
23. Quoted in ibid., 146.
24. Ibid., 175.
25. Thus the title of part 3, chapter 9: see ibid., 252–58.

26. See the remarkable study by Teofilo F. Ruiz, *A King Travels: Festive Traditions in Late Medieval and Early Modern Spain* (Princeton, N.J.: Princeton University Press, 2012), which has the virtue of shifting attention from omnipresent Italy to Spain, then shaking off Muslim domination. Other interesting studies on the festival in the age of the Renaissance include Jean Jacquot, ed., *Les fêtes de la Renaissance*, 3 vols. (Paris: Éditions du CNRS, 1973–75); Michel Plaisance and Françoise Decroisette, eds., *Fêtes urbaines en Italie à l'époque de la Renaissance: Vérone, Florence, Sienne, Naples* (Paris: Klincksieck/Presses de la Sorbonne Nouvelle, 1993); and Roy Strong, *Art and Power: Renaissance Festivals, 1450–1650* (Woodbridge, Suffolk, U.K.: Boydell and Brewer, 1984).

27. See part 6, chapter 1 ("Morality and Religion") in Burckhardt, *The Civilization of the Renaissance in Italy*, 426–43.

28. Ibid., 441.

29. Ibid., 443.

5. THE RENAISSANCE TODAY

1. Among a number of interesting works that I omit to discuss here, two stand out: Peter Burke, *The Italian Renaissance: Culture and Society*, 3rd ed. (Princeton, N.J.: Princeton University Press, 2014); and J. R. Hale, *The Civilization of Europe in the Renaissance* (London: HarperCollins, 1993). In the next chapter I consider a recent book by Robert C. Davis and Beth Lindsmith, *Renaissance People: Lives That Shaped the Modern Age* (London: Thames and Hudson, 2011).

2. Paul Oskar Kristeller, "Lorenzo de' Medici Platonico" [1938], in *Studies in Renaissance Thought and Letters*, 4 vols. (Rome: Edizioni di storia e letteratura, 1956–96), 1:213.

3. Paul Oskar Kristeller, "Un documento sconosciuto sulla giostra di Giuliano de' Medici" [1939], in ibid., 1:437.

4. Eugenio Garin, *Italian Humanism: Philosophy and Civic Life in the Renaissance*, trans. Peter Munz (Oxford: Blackwell, 1965), 3.

5. Ibid., 10.

6. Ibid., 113.

7. Ibid., 221

8. The phrase is due to Augustin Renaudet, quoted in ibid.

9. Thus the title of the opening chapter. See Eugenio Garin, *Medioevo e Rinascimento: Studi e ricerche* (Bari: Laterza, 1954), 13–41.

10. See also in this connection Jean Seznec, *La survivance des dieux antiques: Essai sur le rôle de la tradition mythologique dans l'humanisme et dans l'art de la Renaissance* (London: Warburg Institute, 1940).

11. The *Oxford English Dictionary*'s definition of *periodization* as the division of history in general, and individual historical processes in particular, into "distinguishable portions" is cited in this connection. See Erwin Panofsky, *Renaissance and Renascences in Western Art*, 2 vols. (Stockholm: Almqvist and Wiksell, 1960), 1:1.

12. Panofsky, *Renaissance and Renascences in Western Art*, 1:1. Here Panofsky is quoting an eminent contemporary, the historian Lynn Thorndike.

13. Ibid., 1:11.

14. Quoted in ibid., 1:1.

15. George Boas, "Historical Periods," *Journal of Aesthetics and Art Criticism* 11, no. 3 (1953): 253–54. The most complete survey, astonishing for the number of systems of periodization that have been devised over the centuries, is Johan Hendrik Jacob van der Pot, *De periodisering der geschiedenis: Een overzicht der theorieën* (The Hague: W. P. van Stockum, 1951).

16. Written together with Ronald Lightbown and published by Éditions du Seuil in Paris.
17. See Jean Delumeau, *Une histoire de la Renaissance* (Paris: Perrin, 1999).
18. On festivities in royal and princely contexts see Ruiz, *A King Travels*, esp. 68–112.

6. THE MIDDLE AGES BECOME THE DARK AGES

1. See the article "Reason," in Claude Gauvard, Alain de Libera, and Michel Zink, eds., *Dictionnaire du Moyen Âge* (Paris: Presses Universitaire de France, 2002), 1172.
2. See two books by Chenu that first appeared in 1957, *La théologie au douzième siècle*, 3rd ed. (Paris: Vrin, 1976) and *La théologie comme science au XIIIe siècle*, 3rd ed., rev. and aug. (Paris: Vrin, 1969). The most significant modern work on the importance of reason in the Middle Ages and its various aspects, especially in the thirteenth century, is Alexander Murray, *Reason and Society in the Middle Ages* (Oxford: Clarendon, 1978).
3. See Nicolas Weill-Parot, *Points aveugles de la nature: La rationalité scientifique médiévale face à l'occulte, l'attraction magnétique et l'horreur du vide (XIIIe–milieu du XVe siècle)* (Paris: Les Belles Lettres, 2013).
4. See Girolamo Arnaldi, *Italy and Its Invaders*, trans. Antony Shugaar (Cambridge, Mass.: Harvard University Press, 2005), esp. 124–36.
5. See the various articles on this topic in the featured section "Allemagne, 1500: L'autre Renaissance," *L'Histoire*, no. 387 (May 2013): 38–65.
6. See Étienne Gilson, "Le Moyen Âge comme *saeculum modernum*," in Vittore Branca, ed., *Concetto, storia, miti e immagini del Medio Evo* (Florence: Sansoni, 1973), 1–10.

7. John of Salisbury, *Metalogicon*, 1.3; quoted in ibid., 5. [The English version is taken from J. B. Hall's new translation (Turnhout, Belgium: Brepols, 2013), 131.—Trans.]

8. Quoted in Gilson, "Le Moyen Âge comme *saeculum modernum*," 9.

9. Quoted in John of Salisbury, *Metalogicon*, 3.4. [From the translation by Hall (see note 7 above), 257.—Trans.]

10. Jacques Le Goff, *Intellectuals in the Middle Ages*, trans. Teresa Lavender Fagan (Oxford: Blackwell, 1993), 52. [English version slightly modified, following the form of the original text. The reference is to Anselm's *Cur Deus homo* (Why God Became Man, 1095–98).—Trans.]

11. Quoted in Le Goff, *Intellectuals in the Middle Ages*, 52.

12. Voltaire's remark occurs in the *Essai sur les moeurs* (1756). It is quoted in the article "Scolastique," in Alain Rey, ed., *Dictionnaire culturel en langue française*, 4 vols. (Paris: Le Robert, 2005), 4:632. The author adds: "This judgment of the classical period is totally rejected today."

13. Quoted in "Scolastique," 632.

14. This essay was originally published as a single chapter of a four-volume history of aesthetics, published in Milan by Marzorati in 1959; it was reissued alone three decades later as a short book under the title *Arte e bellezza nell'estetica medievale* (Milan: Bompiani, 1987). The new Italian edition was preceded by the appearance of an English translation, cited below, which, to judge from Eco's remarks in his preface, was the inspiration for it.—Trans.

15. See Umberto Eco, *Art and Beauty in the Middle Ages*, trans. Hugh Bredin (New Haven, Conn.: Yale University Press, 1986), 4–17.

16. The first work seems not to have been translated into English in its entirety; the second has long been available as *The Art of the West in the Middle Ages*, trans. Donald King, 2nd ed., 2 vols. (London: Phaidon, 1969).—Trans.

17. See Alain Erlande-Brandenburg, *La révolution gothique (1130–1190)* (Paris: Picard, 2012).

18. See Gerhart B. Ladner, "Vegetation Symbolism and the Concept of Renaissance," in Millard Meiss, ed., *De artibus opuscula XL: Essays in Honor of Erwin Panofsky*, 2 vols. (New York: New York University Press, 1961), 1:303–22.

19. See Jérôme Baschet, Jean-Claude Bonne, and Pierre-Olivier Dittmar, *Le monde roman: Par-delà le bien et le mal* (Paris: Éditions Arkhê, 2012).

20. Song of Songs 4:12–13. [From the New American Bible, rev. ed. (2011), with slight modifications in closer accordance with the usual French text.—Trans.]

21. See Norbert Elias, *Mozart: Portrait of a Genius*, ed. Michael Schröter, trans. Edmund Jephcott (Berkeley: University of California Press, 1993).

22. See Jean-Patrice Boudet, "La genèse médiévale de la chasse aux sorcières: Jalons en vue d'une relecture," in Nathalie Nabert, ed., *Le mal et le diable: Leurs figures à la fin du Moyen Âge* (Paris: Beauchesne, 1996), 35–52.

23. Davis and Lindsmith, *Renaissance People*, 9.

24. Ibid.

25. See Boucheron, *Histoire du monde au XVᵉ siècle*, 9–29.

26. See Pierre Monnet, "Un empire des couronnes: Royautés électives et unions personnelles au cœur de l'Europe," in ibid., 155–74.

27. See Jean-Philippe Genet, "France, Angleterre, Pays-Bas: L'État moderne," in ibid., 135–54.

7. A LONG MIDDLE AGES

1. Fernand Braudel, *Civilization and Capitalism, 15th–18th Century*, vol. 1, *The Structures of Everyday Life: The Limits of the Possible*, rev. trans. by Siân Reynolds (New York: Harper and Row, 1981), 403.

2. Ibid., 424.
3. Alain Tallon, *L'Europe de la Renaissance* (Paris: Presses Universitaires de France, 2006), 52.
4. See ibid., 60.
5. See Pierre de Jean Olivi, *Traité des contrats*, ed. and trans. Sylvain Piron (Paris: Les Belles Lettres, 2012).
6. Braudel later substantially revised this book as the first part of a three-volume work, now called *Les structures du quotidien: Le possible et l'impossible* (Paris: Armand Colin, 1979), while retaining the original title for the work as a whole. The quotations that follow are taken from Siân Reynolds's translation of the revised edition of the first volume, cited in note 1 above.—Trans.
7. See Braudel, *The Structures of Everyday Life*, 74.
8. See ibid., 104–7.
9. Ibid., 137.
10. Ibid.
11. See ibid., 241.
12. Mathieu Arnoux, "Fer," in Gauvard, Libera, and Zink, *Dictionnaire du Moyen Âge*, 523.
13. Robert Fossier makes this and many other instructive points in *La terre et les hommes en Picardie jusqu'à la fin du XIIIe siècle*, 2 vols. (Paris: B. Nauwelaerts, 1968).
14. This is the second and final volume of Elias's *Über den Prozess der Zivilisation* (Bern: Franke Verlag, 1969), which originally appeared in English as *Power and Civility*, with notes and revisions by the author, as part of *The Civilizing Process*, 2 vols., trans. Edmund Jephcott (New York: Pantheon, 1982). (The first volume was titled *The History of Manners*.) A corrected edition has recently appeared under the title *On the Process of Civilization*, ed. Stephen Mennell, Eric Dunning,

Johan Goudsblom, and Richard Kilminster (Dublin: UCD Press, 2012).—Trans.

15. See Norbert Elias, *The History of Manners*, vol. 1 of *The Civilizing Process*, trans. Edmund Jephcott, 2 vols. (New York: Pantheon, 1982), 84–129.

16. Nathalie Heinich, *La sociologie de Norbert Elias* (Paris: La Découverte, 1997), 10.

17. Franco Cardini, *Europa 1492: Ritratto di un continente cinquecento anni fa* (Milan: Rizzoli, 1989). [Available in English as *Europe 1492: Portrait of a Continent Five Hundred Years Ago*, trans. Jay Hyams (New York: Facts on File, 1989).—Trans.]

18. Bernard Vincent, *1492: L'année admirable* (Paris: Aubier, 1991). [An enlarged edition was issued by Flammarion five years later, but Le Goff cites to the original edition here. No English translation has appeared in the meantime.—Trans.]

19. Cardini, *Europe 1492*, 208–21, 221.

20. Quoted in Vincent, *1492*, 78.

21. See ibid., 72–78.

22. Helen Cooper, *Shakespeare and the Medieval World* (London: Arden Shakespeare, 2010), 1.

23. See ibid., 9–10.

24. See ibid., 12–14, 21–22.

25. Ibid., 52.

26. See ibid., 131–38, 187–91, 28–29.

27. Charles C. Mann, *1493: Uncovering the World Columbus Created* (New York: Knopf, 2011), 5.

28. Ibid., 17.

29. The phrase translates *mal aria*, the Italian source of the English word *malaria*. See ibid., 78–79.—Trans.

30. See ibid., 385–98.

31. On this point and in the discussion that follows I am indebted to a number of the papers presented at a conference on the origins of the modern state organized by the CNRS in Rome, 15–17 October 1984, and subsequently collected in Jean-Philippe Genet, ed., *Culture et idéologie dans la genèse de l'État moderne* (Rome: Ecole française de Rome, 1985).

32. From Jean-Philippe Genet's introductory essay, ibid., 3.

33. See Michael T. Clanchy, *From Memory to Written Record: England, 1066–1307* (Cambridge, Mass.: Harvard University Press, 1979).

34. See Jacques Krynen, "Genèse de l'État et histoire des idées politiques en France à la fin du Moyen Âge," in Genet, *Culture et idéologie dans la genèse de l'État moderne*, 395–412. Roger Chartier notes that Norbert Elias, in his work on the civilizing process, had argued that the modern state was constructed in the West over a period running from the thirteenth century to the eighteenth; see "Construction de l'État moderne et formes culturelles: Perspectives et questions," in ibid., 491–503.

35. See Michel Pastoureau, "L'État et son image emblématique," in ibid., 145–53.

36. See the recent study of this cycle in Patrick Boucheron, *Conjurer la peur: Sienne, 1338. Essai sur la force politique des images* (Paris: Seuil, 2013).

37. See Jean-Louis Biget, Jean-Claude Hervé, and Yvon Thébert, "Expressions iconographiques et monumentales du pouvoir d'État en France et en Espagne à la fin du Moyen Âge: L'exemple d'Albi et de Grenade," in Genet, *Culture et idéologie dans la genèse de l'État moderne*, 245–79.

38. Carlo M. Cipolla, *Before the Industrial Revolution: European Society and Economy, 1000–1700*, 3rd ed. (New York: Norton, 1994), 100.

39. The phrase occurs in Mirabeau's *L'ami des hommes, ou traité sur la population*, written in 1756 and published the following year.—Trans.

40. See David Garrioch, *The Making of Revolutionary Paris* (Berkeley: University of California Press, 2002).

41. From Antoine de Baecque's review of the French edition of Garrioch's book in *Le Monde des livres*, 9 May 2013, 2.

42. See "La génie de la Renaissance: Quand l'Europe se réinvente," special issue, *Les Cahiers de science & vie*, no. 128 (April 2012).

43. See, for example, Beryl Smalley, "Ecclesiastical Attitudes to Novelty, c. 1100–c. 1250," in Derek Baker, ed., *Church, Society, and Politics*, Studies in Church History, vol. 12 (Oxford: Basil Blackwell, 1975), 113–31.

44. The emphasis in each case is mine.

CONCLUSION

1. See, for example, Patrick Manning, *Navigating World History: Historians Create a Global Past* (New York: Palgrave Macmillan, 2003); and Romain Bertrand, "Histoire globale, histoire connectée," in Delacroix, Dosse, Garcia, and Offenstadt, *Historiographies*, 1:366–77.

BIBLIOGRAPHY

"Allemagne, 1500: L'autre Renaissance." *L'Histoire*, no. 387 (May 2013): 38–65.

Allier, Éric. *Les temps capitaux*. Vol. 1, *Récits de la conquête du temps*. Paris: Le Cerf, 1991.

Altavista, Clara. *Lucca e Paolo Guinigi (1400–1430): La costruzione di une corte rinascimentale. Città, architettura, arte*. Pisa: ETS, 2005.

Amalvi, Christian. *De l'art et la manière d'accommoder les héros de l'histoire de France: Essais de mythologie nationale*. Paris: Albin Michel, 1988.

Angenendt, Arnold. *Heiligen und Reliquien: Die Geschichte ihres Kultes vom frühen Christentum bis zum Gegenwart*. Munich: Beck, 1994.

Arnaldi, Girolamo. *L'Italia e i suoi invasori*. Rome: Laterza, 2002.

Arnoux, Mathieu. "Fer." In Gauvard, Libera, and Zink, *Dictionnaire du Moyen Âge*, 523–24.

Aubert, Marcel. "Le romantisme et le Moyen Âge." In *Le romantisme et l'art* (Paris: Laurens, 1928), 23–48.

Autrand, Michel, ed. *L'image du Moyen Âge dans la littérature française de la Renaissance au XXᵉ siècle*. Double issue of *La Licorne* 6, nos. 1–2 (1982).

Aymard, Maurice. "La transizione dal feudalismo al capitalismo." In *Storia d'Italia, Annali*, vol. 1, *Dal feudalismo al capitalismo*, 1131–92. Turin: Einaudi, 1978.

Baschet, Jérôme. *La civilisation féodale: De l'an mil à la colonisation de l'Amérique*. Paris: Aubier, 2004.

Baschet, Jérôme, Jean-Claude Bonne, and Pierre-Olivier Dittmar. *Le monde roman: Par-delà le bien et le mal*. Paris: Éditions Arkhê, 2012.

Beauvais, Michel. *1492: L'Europe au temps de la découverte de l'Amérique*. Paris: Solar, 1990. Adapted and translated by Franco Cardini as *Europa 1492: Ritratto di un continente cinquecento anni fa*. Florence: Rizzoli, 2000.

Bec, Christian. *Florence, 1300–1600: Histoire et culture*. Nancy: Presses Universitaires de Nancy, 1986.

Bec, Christian, Ivan Cloulas, Bertrand Jestaz, and Alberto Tenenti. *L'Italie de la Renaissance: Un monde en mutation, 1378–1494*. Paris: Fayard, 1990.

Below, Georg von. *Über Historische Periodisierungen mit besonderem Blick auf die Grenze zwischen Mittelalter und Neuzeit*. Berlin: Deutsche Verlagsgesellschaft für Politik und Geschichte, 1925.

Berlinger, Rudolph. "Le temps et l'homme chez Saint Augustin." *L'année théologique augustinienne* 13 (1953): 260–79.

Bertrand, Romain. "Histoire globale, histoire connectée." In Delacroix, Dosse, Garcia, and Offenstadt, *Historiographies*, 1:366–77.

Biget, Jean-Louis, Jean-Claude Hervé, and Yvon Thébert. "Expressions iconographiques et monumentales du pouvoir d'État en France et en Espagne à la fin du Moyen Âge: L'exemple d'Albi et de Grenade." In Genet, *Culture et idéologie dans la genèse de l'État moderne*, 245–79.

Boas, George. "Historical Periods." *Journal of Aesthetics and Art Criticism* 11, no. 3 (1953): 248–54.

Boucheron, Patrick. *Conjurer la peur: Sienne, 1338. Essai sur la force politique des images.* Paris: Seuil, 2013.

——, ed. *Histoire du monde au XVᵉ siècle.* Paris: Fayard, 2009.

Boudet, Jean-Patrice. "La genèse médievale de la chasse aux sorcières: Jalons en vue d'une relecture." In Nathalie Nabert, ed., *Le mal et le diable: Leurs figures à la fin du Moyen Âge*, 35–52. Paris: Beauchesne, 1996.

Bouwsma, William J. *Venice and the Defense of Republican Liberty: Renaissance Values in the Age of the Counter Reformation.* Berkeley: University of California Press, 1968.

Branca, Vittore, ed. *Concetto, storia, miti et immagini del Medio Evo.* Florence: Sansoni, 1973.

Braudel, Fernand. *Civilisation matérielle et capitalisme, XVᵉ–XVIIIᵉ siècles.* Paris: Armand Colin, 1967. Revised edition published as *Les structures du quotidien: Le possible et l'impossible* (Paris: Armand Colin, 1979).

——. "Histoire et sciences sociales: La longue durée." *Annales ESC* 13, no. 4 (1958): 725–53. Reprinted in *Écrits sur l'histoire* (Paris: Flammarion, 1969), 41–83.

Brioist, Pascal. *La Renaissance, 1470–1570.* Paris: Atlande, 2003.

Brown, Judith C. "Prosperity or Hard Times in Renaissance Italy?" *Renaissance Quarterly* 42, no. 4 (1989): 761–80.

Bruter, Annie. *L'histoire enseignée au Grand Siècle: Naissance d'une pédagogie.* Paris: Belin, 1998.

Burckhardt, Jacob. *The Civilization of the Renaissance in Italy.* Translated by S. G. C. Middlemore. New York: Harper and Row, 1958.

——. *La civilisation de la Renaissance en Italie.* Translated by Henri Schmitt. Revised and corrected by Robert Klein. Paris: Bartillat, 2012.

Burke, Peter. *The European Renaissance: Centres and Peripheries*. London: Wiley-Blackwell, 1998.

——. *The Italian Renaissance: Culture and Society*. 3rd ed. Princeton, N.J.: Princeton University Press, 2014.

——. *The Renaissance Sense of the Past*. London: Edward Arnold, 1969.

Burr, George L. "How the Middle Ages Got Their Name." *American Historical Review* 20, no. 4 (1915): 838–40.

Campbell, Lorne. *Renaissance Portraits: European Portrait Painting in the 14th, 15th, and 16th Centuries*. New Haven, Conn.: Yale University Press, 1990.

Cardini, Franco. *Europa 1492: Ritratto di un continente cinquecento anni fa*. Milan: Rizzoli, 1989.

Castelfranchi Vegas, Liana. *Italie et Flandres: Primitifs flamands et Renaissance italienne*. Paris: L'Aventurine, 1995.

Chaix, Gérald. *La Renaissance des années 1470 aux années 1560*. Paris: Sedes, 2002.

Chaix-Ruy, Jules. "Le problème du temps dans les *Confessions* et dans la *Cité de Dieu*," *Giornale di Metafisica* 9 (1954): 464–77.

——. *Saint Augustin: Temps et histoire*. Paris: Études Augustiniennes, 1956.

Chartier, Roger. "Construction de l'État moderne et formes culturelles: Perspectives et questions." In Genet, *Culture et idéologie dans la genèse de l'État moderne*, 491–503.

Chaunu, Pierre. *Colomb ou la logique de l'imprévisible*. Paris: François Bourin, 1993.

Chenu, Marie-Dominique. *La théologie au douzième siècle*. Paris: Vrin, 1957; 3rd ed., 1976.

——. *La théologie comme science au XIIIe siècle*. Paris: Vrin, 1957; 3rd ed., revised and augmented, 1969.

Cipolla, Carlo M. *Before the Industrial Revolution; European Society and Economy, 1000–1700*. 3rd ed. New York: Norton, 1994.

Clanchy, Michael T. *From Memory to Written Record: England, 1066–1307.* Cambridge, Mass.: Harvard University Press, 1979.

Clark, Kenneth. *The Gothic Revival: A Study in the History of Taste.* London: Constable, 1928.

Cloulas, Ivan. *Charles VIII et le mirage italien.* Paris: Albin Michel, 1986.

Cochrane, Eric. *Historians and Historiography in the Italian Renaissance.* Chicago: University of Chicago Press, 1981.

Connell, William J. *Society and Individual in Renaissance Florence.* Berkeley: University of California Press, 2002.

Contamine, Philippe, ed. *Guerres et concurrence entre les États européens du XIVe au XVIIIe siècle.* Paris: Presses Universitaires de France, 1998.

Conti, Alessandro. "L'evoluzione dell'artista." In Giovanni Previtali, ed., *Storia dell'arte italiana.* Vol. 2, *L'artista et il pubblico,* 117–264. Turin: Einaudi, 1979.

Cooper, Helen. *Shakespeare and the Medieval World.* London: Arden Shakespeare, 2010.

Corbellari, Alain, and Christopher Lucken, eds. "Lire le Moyen Âge?" Special issue of *Equinoxe* 16 (Fall 1996).

Cosenza, Mario Emilio. *Biographical and Bibliographical Dictionary of the Italian Humanists and of the World of Scholarship in Italy, 1300–1800.* 2nd ed. Revised and augmented. 7 vols. Boston: G. K. Hall, 1962–68.

Crouzet-Pavan, Elisabeth, ed. *Pouvoir et édilité: Les grands chantiers dans l'Italie communale et seigneuriale.* Rome: École française de Rome, 2003.

——. *Renaissances italiennes, 1380–1500.* Paris: Albin Michel, 2007.

Cullmann, Oscar. *Christ et le temps.* Neuchâtel: Delachaux et Niestlé, 1947.

Dainville, François de. *L'éducation des jésuites (XVIe–XVIIIe siècle).* Paris: Minuit, 1978.

Daussy, Hugues, Patrick Gilli, and Michel Nassiet. *La Renaissance, vers 1470–vers 1560.* Paris: Belin, 2003.

Davis, Robert C., and Beth Lindsmith. *Renaissance People: Lives That Shaped the Modern Age*. London: Thames and Hudson, 2011.

Delacroix, Christian, François Dosse, Patrick Garcia, and Nicolas Offenstadt, eds. *Historiographies: Concepts et débats*. 2 vols. Paris: Gallimard, 2010.

Delumeau, Jean. *La peur en Occident, XIVe–XVIIIe siècles*. Paris: Fayard, 1978.

——. *Une histoire de la Renaissance*. Paris: Perrin, 1999.

Delumeau, Jean, and R. W. Lightbown. *La Renaissance*. Paris: Seuil, 1996.

Demurger, Alain. *Temps de crises, temps d'espoirs, XIVe–XVe siècles*. Paris: Seuil, 1990.

Dhotel, Jean-Claude. *Les origines du catéchisme moderne d'après les premiers manuels imprimés en France*. Paris: Aubier-Montaigne, 1967.

Duby, Georges. *Le temps des cathédrales: L'art et société, 980–1420*. Paris: Gallimard, 1976.

——. *L'histoire continue*. Paris: Odile Jacob, 1991.

Dumoulin, Olivier, and Raphaël Valéry, eds. *Périodes: La construction du temps historique*. Paris: Éditions de l'EHESS, 1991.

Dunn-Lardeau, Brenda, ed. *Entre la lumière et les ténèbres: Aspects du Moyen Âge et de la Renaissance dans la culture des XIXe et XXe siècles*. Paris: Champion, 1999.

Eco, Umberto. *Art and Beauty in the Middle Ages*. Translated by Hugh Bredin. New Haven, Conn.: Yale University Press, 1986.

——. "Dieci modi di sognare il medio evo." In *Sugli specchi e altri saggi*, 78–89. Milan: Bompiani, 1985.

Edelman, Nathan. *Attitudes of Seventeenth-Century France Toward the Middle Ages*. New York: King's Crown Press, 1946.

Elias, Norbert. *Mozart: Portrait of a Genius*. Edited by Michael Schröter. Translated by Edmund Jephcott. Berkeley: University of California Press, 1993.

———. *On the Process of Civilization*. Translated by Edmund Jephcott. Revised and edited by Stephen Mennell, Eric Dunning, Johan Goudsblom, and Richard Kilminster. Dublin: UCD Press, 2012.

Epstein, S. A. *Genoa and the Genoese, 958–1528*. Chapel Hill: University of North Carolina Press, 1996.

Erlande-Brandenburg, Alain. *La révolution gothique (1130–1190)*. Paris: Picard, 2012.

Falco, Giorgio. *La polemica sul medio evo*. Turin: Società industriale grafica Fedetto, 1933.

Febvre, Lucien. "Comment Jules Michelet inventa la Renaissance." In *Studi in onore di Gino Luzzatto*. 4 vols. Milan: A. Giuffrè, 1950, 3:1–11. Reprinted in Lucien Febvre, *Pour une histoire à part entière* (Paris: SEVPEN, 1962), 717–29; and in *Le genre humain* 27 (June 1993): 77–87.

Ferguson, Wallace K. *The Renaissance in Historical Thought: Five Centuries of Interpretation*. Boston: Houghton Mifflin, 1948.

Focillon, Henri. *Art d'Occident: Le Moyen Âge roman et gothique*. Paris: A. Colin, 1938.

———. *L'art des sculpteurs romans: Recherches sur l'histoire des formes*. Paris: E. Leroux, 1931.

Fossier, Robert. *La terre et les hommes en Picardie jusqu'à la fin du XIIIe siècle*. 2 vols. Paris: B. Nauwelaerts, 1968.

Fumaroli, Marc. "Aux origines de la connaissance historique du Moyen Âge: Humanisme, réforme et gallicanisme au XVIe siècle." *XVIIe siècle* 114/115 (1977): 5–30.

Garcia, Patrick, and Jean Leduc. "Enseignement de l'histoire en France." In Delacroix, Dosse, Garcia, and Offenstadt, *Historiographies*, 1:104–11.

Garin, Eugenio. *L'educazione in Europa, 1400–1600*. Rome: Laterza, 1976.

——. *L'umanesimo italiano: Filosofia e vita civile nel Rinascimento*. 2nd ed. Bari: Laterza, 1965. [First Italian edition, 1952; originally published in German as *Der italienische Humanismus* (Bern: A. Franke, 1947).]

——. *Medioevo e Rinascimento: Studi e ricerche*. Bari: Laterza, 1954.

——. "Medio Evo e tempi bui: Concetto e polemiche nella storia del pensiero dal XV al XVIII secolo." In Branca, *Concetto, storia, miti e immagini del Medio Evo*, 199–224.

Garrioch, David. *The Making of Revolutionary Paris*. Berkeley: University of California Press, 2002.

Gauvard, Claude, Alain de Libera, and Michel Zink, eds. *Dictionnaire du Moyen Âge*. Paris: Presses Universitaires de France, 2002.

Genet, Jean-Philippe, ed. *Culture et idéologie dans la genèse de l'État moderne*. Rome: École française de Rome, 1985.

——. "France, Angleterre, Pays-Bas: L'État moderne." In Boucheron, *Histoire du monde au XVᵉ siècle*, 135–54.

Ghelardi, Maurizio, and Matthias Waschek, eds. *Relire Burckhardt*. Lectures delivered at the Musée du Louvre. Paris: École nationale supérieure des beaux-arts, 1997.

Gibert, Pierre. *La Bible à la naissance de l'histoire: Au temps de Saül, David et Salomon*. Paris: Fayard, 1979.

Gibert, Pierre, and Christoph Théobald, eds. *Théologies et vérité au défi de l'histoire*. Leuven: Peeters, 2010.

Gilson, Étienne. "Le Moyen Âge comme *saeculum modernum*." In Branca, *Concetto, storia, miti e immagini del Medio Evo*, 1–10.

Gossman, Lionel. *Medievalism and the Ideologies of the Enlightenment: The World and Work of La Curne de Sainte-Palaye*. Baltimore: Johns Hopkins University Press, 1968.

Greenblatt, Stephen. *Renaissance Self-Fashioning: From More to Shakespeare*. Chicago: University of Chicago Press, 1980.

Guenée, Bernard, ed. *Études sur l'historiographie médiévale*. Paris: Publications de la Sorbonne, 1977.

———. "Histoire." In Le Goff and Schmitt, *Dictionnaire raisonné de l'Occident médiéval*, 483–96.

———. *Histoire et culture historique dans l'Occident médiéval*. Paris: Aubier Montaigne, 1980.

Guichemerre, Roger. "L'image du Moyen Âge chez les écrivains français du XVIIe siècle." In Michel Perrin, ed., *Dire le Moyen Âge, hier et aujourd'hui*, 189–210. Paris: Université de Picardie/Presses Universitaires de France, 1990.

Guitton, J. *Le temps et l'éternité chez Plotin et Saint Augustin*. Paris: Vrin, 1971.

Hale, J. R. *The Civilization of Europe in the Renaissance*. London: Harper Collins, 1993.

Hartog, François. *Croire en l'histoire*. Paris: Flammarion, 2013.

———. *Évidence de l'histoire: Ce que voient les historiens*. Paris: Éditions de l'EHESS, 2005.

———. *Le miroir d'Hérodote: Essai sur la représentation de l'autre*. Paris: Gallimard, 1980.

———, ed. *L'histoire d'Homère à Augustin*. Translated by Michel Casevitz. Paris: Seuil, 1999.

———. "Ordre des temps: Chronographie, chronologie, histoire." In Gibert and Théobald, *Théologies et vérité au défi de l'histoire*, 279–89.

———. *Régimes d'historicité: Présentisme et expériences du temps*. Paris: Seuil, 2003.

Haskins, Charles H. *The Renaissance of the Twelfth Century*. Cambridge, Mass.: Harvard University Press, 1927.

Hauser, Henri. *La modernité du XVIe siècle*. Paris: Alcan, 1939.

Heer, Friedrich. "Die Renaissance Ideologie im frühen Mittelalter."

Mitteilungen des Instituts für Osterreichische Geschichtsforschung 57 (1949): 23–81.

Heinich, Nathalie. *La sociologie de Norbert Elias*. Paris: La Découverte, 1997.

Huizinga, Johan. *L'automne du Moyen Âge*. Translated by J. Bastin. Preface by Jacques Le Goff. Paris: Payot, 1975. [Reissued in 2002 with an interview between Jacques Le Goff and Claude Mettra.]

Jacquot, Jean, ed. *Les fêtes de la Renaissance*. 3 vols. Paris: Éditions du CNRS, 1973–75.

John of Salisbury. *Metalogicon*. Introduction by J. P. Haseldine. Translated by J. B. Hall. Turnhout, Belgium: Brepols, 2013.

Jones, Philip. *The Italian City-State: From Commune to Signoria*. Oxford: Clarendon, 1997.

Jouanna, Arlette, Philippe Hamon, Dominique Biloghi, and Guy Le Thiec. *La France de la Renaissance: Histoire et dictionnaire*. Paris: Laffont, 2001.

Koselleck, Reinhart. *L'expérience de l'histoire*. Edited by Michael Werner. Translated by Alexandre Escudier. Paris: Gallimard/Seuil, 1997.

Kristeller, Paul Oskar. *Medieval Aspects of Renaissance Learning: Three Essays*. Durham, N.C.: Duke University Press, 1974.

——. *Renaissance Philosophy and the Medieval Tradition*. Latrobe, Pa.: Archabbey Press, 1966.

——. *Studies in Renaissance Thought and Letters*. 4 vols. Rome: Edizioni di storia e letteratura, 1956–1996.

Krynen, Jacques. "Genèse de l'État et histoire des idées politiques en France à la fin du Moyen Âge." In Genet, *Culture et idéologie dans la genèse de l'État moderne*, 395–412.

Ladner, Gerhart B. "Vegetation Symbolism and the Concept of Renaissance." In Millard Meiss, ed., *De artibus opuscula XL: Essays in Honor of Erwin Panofsky*. 2 vols. 1:303–22. New York: New York University Press, 1961.

"La génie de la Renaissance: Quand l'Europe se réinvente," special issue, *Les Cahiers de science & vie*, no. 128 (April 2012).

Lançon, Bertrand. *L'Antiquité tardive*. Paris: Presses Universitaires de France, 1997.

La Roncière, Monique de, and Michel Mollat du Jourdin. *Les Portulans: Cartes marines du XIIIᵉ–XVIIᵉ siècle*. Paris: Nathan, 1984.

Leduc, Jean. *Les historiens et le temps: Conceptions, problématiques, écritures*. Paris: Seuil, 1999.

——. "Période, périodisation." In Delacroix, Dosse, Garcia, and Offenstadt, *Historiographies*, 2:830–38.

Le Goff, Jacques. *À la recherche du temps sacré: Jacques de Voragine et la Légende dorée*. Paris: Perrin, 2011.

——. *Histoire et mémoire*. Paris: Gallimard, 1988.

——. *Les intellectuels au Moyen Âge*. Paris: Seuil, 1957.

——. *L'imaginaire médiéval*. Paris: Gallimard, 1985.

——. *Pour un autre Moyen Âge: Temps, travail et culture en Occident*. Paris: Gallimard, 1977.

——. "Temps." In Le Goff and Schmitt, *Dictionnaire raisonné de l'Occident médiéval*, 1113–22.

——. *Un long Moyen Âge*. Paris: Tallandier, 2004.

Le Goff, Jacques, and Jean-Claude Schmitt, eds. *Dictionnaire raisonné de l'Occident médiéval*. Paris: Fayard, 1999.

Le Pogam, Pierre-Yves, and Audrey Bodéré-Clergeau. *Le temps à l'œuvre*. Catalogue of an exhibit at the Musée du Louvre in Lens (December 2012–October 2013). Lens: Éditions Invenit–Louvre-Lens, 2012.

Le Roy Ladurie, Emmanuel. "Un concept: L'unification microbienne du monde (XIVᵉ–XVIIᵉ siècles)." *Revue suisse de l'histoire* 23, no. 4 (1973): 627–96.

Liebeschütz, Hans. *Medieval Humanism in the Life and Writings of John of Salisbury*. London: Warburg Institute, 1950.

Lopez, Robert S. "Still Another Renaissance?" *American Historical Review* 57 (1951): 1–21.

Luneau, Auguste. *L'histoire du salut chez les Pères de l'Église: La doctrine des âges du monde*. Paris: Beauchesne, 1964.

Mahn-Lot, Marianne. *Portrait historique de Christophe Colomb*. Paris: Seuil, 1960.

Maire Vigueur, Jean-Claude, ed. *D'une ville à l'autre: Structures matérielles et organisation de l'espace dans les villes européennes, XIIIe–XVIe siècles*. Rome: École française de Rome, 1989.

Mann, Charles C. *1493: Uncovering the World Columbus Created*. New York: Knopf, 2011.

Manning, Patrick. *Navigating World History: Historians Create a Global Past*. New York: Palgrave Macmillan, 2003.

Marrou, Henri-Irénée. *L'ambivalence du temps de l'histoire chez Saint Augustin*. Paris: Institut d'études médiévales/Vrin, 1950.

Melis, Federigo. *I mercanti italiani nell'Europa medievale e rinanscimentale*. Florence: Le Monnier, 1990.

Meyer, Jean. *Histoire du sucre*. Paris: Desjonquères, 1989.

Michelet, Jules. *Cours au Collège de France, 1838–1851*. Edited by Paul Viallaneix. 2 vols. Paris: Gallimard, 1995.

——. *Histoire de France*. Vols. 4–8 in *Œuvres complètes*. Edited by Paul Viallaneix. 21 vols. Paris: Flammarion, 1971–87.

Milo, Daniel S. *Trahir le temps*. Paris: Les Belles Lettres, 1991.

Mollat, Michel. "Y a-t-il une économie de la Renaissance?" In *Actes du colloque sur la Renaissance*, 37–54. Paris: Vrin, 1958.

Momigliano, Arnaldo D. "Ancient History and the Antiquarian." In *Studies in Historiography*, 1–39. London: Weidenfeld and Nicolson, 1966.

———. *Tra storia e storicismo*. Pisa: Nistri-Lischi, 1985.

Mommsen, Theodor E. "Petrarch's Conception of the Dark Ages." *Speculum* 17 (1942): 126–42.

Monnet, Pierre. "Un empire des couronnes: Royautés électives et unions personnelles au cœur de l'Europe." In Boucheron, *Histoire du monde au XVᵉ siècle*, 155–74.

Moos, Peter von. "Muratori et les origines du médiévisme italien." *Romania* 114 (1996): 203–24.

Murray, Alexander. *Reason and Society in the Middle Ages*. Oxford: Clarendon, 1978.

Neveux, Hugues, Jean Jacquart, and Emmanuel Le Roy Ladurie. *L'âge classique des paysans, 1340–1789*. Vol. 2 of Georges Duby and Armand Wallon, eds., *Histoire de la France rurale*. Paris: Seuil, 1975.

Nitze, William A. "The So-Called Twelfth Century Renaissance." *Speculum* 23 (1948): 464–71.

Nolhac, Pierre de. *Pétrarque et l'humanisme*. 2nd ed. Paris: Champion, 1907.

Nordström, Johan. *Moyen Âge et Renaissance*. Translated by T. Hammar. Paris: Stock, 1933.

Norel, Philippe. *L'histoire économique globale*. Paris: Seuil, 2009.

Olivi, Pierre de Jean. *Traité des contrats* [c. 1292]. Edited and translated by Sylvain Piron. Paris: Les Belles Lettres, 2012.

Panofsky, Erwin. *Renaissance and Renascences in Western Art*. 2 vols. Stockholm: Almqvist and Wiksell, 1960.

Paravicini Bagliani, Agostino. "Âges de vie." In Le Goff and Schmitt, *Dictionnaire raisonné de l'Occident médiéval*, 7–19.

Pastoureau, Michel. "L'État et son image emblématique." In Genet, *Culture et idéologie dans la genèse de l'État moderne*, 145–53.

Patzelt, Erna. *Die Karolingische Renaissance*. Vienna: Österreichischer Schulbücherverlag, 1924.

"Périodisation en histoire des sciences et de la philosophie." Special issue of *Revue de synthèse*, no. 3–4 (1987).

Plaisance, Michel, and Françoise Decroisette, eds. *Fêtes urbaines en Italie à l'époque de la Renaissance: Vérone, Florence, Sienne, Naples*. Paris: Klincksieck/Presses de la Sorbonne Nouvelle, 1993.

Pomian, Krzysztof. *L'ordre du temps*. Paris: Gallimard, 1984.

Pot, Johan Hendrik Jacob van der. *De periodisering der geschiedenis: Een overzicht der theorieën*. The Hague: W. P. van Stockum, 1951.

Poulet, Georges. *Études sur le temps humain*. Vol. 1. Paris: Plon, 1949.

Poussou, Jean-Pierre, ed. *La Renaissance, des années 1470 aux années 1560: Enjeux historiographiques, méthodologie, bibliographie commentée*. Paris: Armand Colin, 2002.

Renaudet, Augustin. "Autour d'une définition de l'humanisme." *Bibliothèque d'Humanisme et Renaissance* 6 (1945): 7–49.

Renucci, Paul. *L'aventure de l'humanisme européen au Moyen Âge, IVᵉ–XIVᵉ siècles*. Paris: Les Belles Lettres, 1953.

Ribémont, Bernard, ed. *Le temps, sa mesure et sa perception au Moyen Âge*. Caen: Paradigme, 1992.

Ricoeur, Paul. *La mémoire, l'histoire, l'oubli*. Paris: Seuil, 2000.

——. *Temps et récit*. 3 vols. Paris: Seuil, 1983–85.

Romani, Ruggiero, and Alberto Tenenti. *Die Grundlegung der modernen Welt*. Frankfurt: Fischer Verlag, 1967. [Simultaneously published in Italian as *Alle origini del mondo moderno (1350–1550)*. Milan: Feltrinelli, 1967.]

Ruiz, Teofilo F. *A King Travels: Festive Traditions in Late Medieval and Early Modern Spain*. Princeton, N.J.: Princeton University Press, 2012.

Schild Bunim, Miriam. *Space in Medieval Painting and the Forerunners of Perspective*. New York: Columbia University Press, 1940.

Schmidt, Roderich. "Aetates Mundi: Die Weltalter als Gliederungsprinzip der Geschichte." *Zeitschrift für Kirchengeschichte* 67 (1955–56): 288–317.

Schmitt, Jean-Claude. "L'imaginaire du temps dans l'histoire chrétienne." *Pris-Ma* 25, no. 49–50 (2009): 135–59.

Seznec, Jean. *La survivance des dieux antiques: Essai sur le rôle de la tradition mythologique dans l'humanisme et dans l'art de la Renaissance.* London: Warburg Institute, 1940.

Simoncini, Giorgio. "La persistenza del gotico dopo il medioevo: Periodizzazione ed orientamente figurativi." In Giorgio Simoncini, ed., *La tradizione medievale nell'architettura italiana,* 1–24. Florence: Olschki, 1992.

Singer, Samuel. "Karolingische Renaissance." *Germanisch-Romanische Monatsschrift* 13 (1925): 187–201, 243–58.

Smalley, Beryl. "Ecclesiastical Attitudes to Novelty, c. 1100–c. 1250." In Derek Baker, ed., *Church, Society, and Politics,* 113–31. Studies in Church History, vol. 12. Oxford: Basil Blackwell, 1975.

Strong, Roy. *Art and Power: Renaissance Festivals, 1450–1650.* Woodbridge, U.K.: Boydell and Brewer, 1984.

Tallon, Alain. *L'Europe de la Renaissance.* Paris: Presses Universitaires de France, 2006.

Taviani, Paolo Emilio. *Cristoforo Colombo: La genesi della granda scoperta.* 2 vols. Novara: De Agostini, 1974.

Toubert, Pierre, and Michel Zink, eds. *Moyen Âge et Renaissance au Collège de France.* Paris: Fayard, 2009.

Ullmann, Walter. *Medieval Foundations of Renaissance Humanism.* Ithaca, N.Y.: Cornell University Press, 1977.

——. "The Medieval Origins of the Renaissance." In André Chastel, ed., *The Renaissance: Essays in Interpretation,* 33–82. London: Methuen, 1982.

Vincent, Bernard. *1492: L'année admirable.* Paris: Aubier, 1991.

Voltaire. *The Age of Louis XIV.* Translated by William H. Fleming. Vol. 12 of *The Works of Voltaire.* New York: E. R. DuMont, 1901.

Voss, Jürgen. *Das Mittelalter im historischen Denken Frankreichs: Untersuchungen zur Geschichte des Mittelaltersbegriffs und Mittelalterbewertung von der zweiten Hälfte des 16. bis zur Mitte des 19. Jahrhunderts*. Munich: Fink, 1972.

Ward, Patricia A. *The Medievalism of Victor Hugo*. University Park: Pennsylvania State University Press, 1975.

Weill-Parot, Nicolas. *Points aveugles de la nature: La rationalité scientifique médiévale face à l'occulte, l'attraction magnétique et l'horreur du vide (XIIIᵉ–milieu du XVᵉ siècle)*. Paris: Les Belles Lettres, 2013.

Werner, Ernst. "De l'esclavage à la féodalité: La périodisation de l'histoire mondiale." *Annales ESC* 17, no. 5 (1962): 930–39.

Wittkower, Rudolf, and Margot Wittkower. *Born Under Saturn: The Character and Conduct of Artists; A Documented History from Antiquity to the French Revolution*. New York: Random House, 1963.

Zorzi, Andrea. "La politique criminelle en Italie, XIIIᵉ–XVIIᵉ siècles." *Crime, histoire et sociétés* 2, no. 2 (1988): 91–110.

Zumthor, Paul. "Le Moyen Âge de Victor Hugo." Preface to Victor Hugo, *Notre-Dame de Paris*. Paris: Le club français du livre, 1967.

——. *Parler du Moyen Âge*. Paris: Minuit, 1980.

INDEX

EUROPEAN PERSPECTIVES

A Series in Social Thought and Cultural Criticism

Lawrence D. Kritzman, *Editor*

Gilles Deleuze, *The Logic of Sense*

Julia Kristeva, *Strangers to Ourselves*

Theodor W. Adorno, *Notes to Literature*, vols. 1 and 2

Richard Wolin, ed., *The Heidegger Controversy*

Antonio Gramsci, *Prison Notebooks*, vols. 1, 2, and 3

Jacques Le Goff, *History and Memory*

Alain Finkielkraut, *Remembering in Vain: The Klaus Barbie Trial and Crimes Against Humanity*

Julia Kristeva, *Nations Without Nationalism*

Pierre Bourdieu, *The Field of Cultural Production*

Pierre Vidal-Naquet, *Assassins of Memory: Essays on the Denial of the Holocaust*

Hugo Ball, *Critique of the German Intelligentsia*

Gilles Deleuze, *Logic and Sense*

Gilles Deleuze and Félix Guattari, *What Is Philosophy?*

Karl Heinz Bohrer, *Suddenness: On the Moment of Aesthetic Appearance*

Julia Kristeva, *Time and Sense: Proust and the Experience of Literature*

Alain Finkielkraut, *The Defeat of the Mind*

Julia Kristeva, *New Maladies of the Soul*

Elisabeth Badinter, *XY: On Masculine Identity*

Karl Löwith, *Martin Heidegger and European Nihilism*

Gilles Deleuze, *Negotiations, 1972–1990*

Pierre Vidal-Naquet, *The Jews: History, Memory, and the Present*

Norbert Elias, *The Germans*

Louis Althusser, *Writings on Psychoanalysis: Freud and Lacan*

Elisabeth Roudinesco, *Jacques Lacan: His Life and Work*

Ross Guberman, *Julia Kristeva Interviews*

Kelly Oliver, *The Portable Kristeva*

Pierre Nora, *Realms of Memory: The Construction of the French Past*
    Vol. 1: *Conflicts and Divisions*
    Vol. 2: *Traditions*
    Vol. 3: *Symbols*

Claudine Fabre-Vassas, *The Singular Beast: Jews, Christians, and the Pig*

Paul Ricoeur, *Critique and Conviction: Conversations with François Azouvi and Marc de Launay*

Theodor W. Adorno, *Critical Models: Interventions and Catchwords*

Alain Corbin, *Village Bells: Sound and Meaning in the Nineteenth-Century French Countryside*

Zygmunt Bauman, *Globalization: The Human Consequences*

Emmanuel Levinas, *Entre Nous: Essays on Thinking-of-the-Other*

Jean-Louis Flandrin and Massimo Montanari, *Food: A Culinary History*

Tahar Ben Jelloun, *French Hospitality: Racism and North African Immigrants*

Emmanuel Levinas, *Alterity and Transcendence*

Sylviane Agacinski, *Parity of the Sexes*

Alain Finkielkraut, *In the Name of Humanity: Reflections on the Twentieth Century*

Julia Kristeva, *The Sense and Non-sense of Revolt: The Powers and Limits of Psychoanalysis*

Régis Debray, *Transmitting Culture*

Catherine Clément and Julia Kristeva, *The Feminine and the Sacred*

Alain Corbin, *The Life of an Unknown: The Rediscovered World of a Clog Maker in Nineteenth-Century France*

Michel Pastoureau, *The Devil's Cloth: A History of Stripes and Striped Fabric*

Julia Kristeva, *Hannah Arendt*

Carlo Ginzburg, *Wooden Eyes: Nine Reflections on Distance*

Elisabeth Roudinesco, *Why Psychoanalysis?*

Alain Cabantous, *Blasphemy: Impious Speech in the West from the Seventeenth to the Nineteenth Century*

Luce Irigaray, *Between East and West: From Singularity to Community*

Julia Kristeva, *Melanie Klein*

Gilles Deleuze, *Dialogues II*

Julia Kristeva, *Intimate Revolt: The Powers and Limits of Psychoanalysis, vol. 2*

Claudia Benthien, *Skin: On the Cultural Border Between Self and the World*

Sylviane Agacinski, *Time Passing: Modernity and Nostalgia*

Emmanuel Todd, *After the Empire: The Breakdown of the American Order*

Hélène Cixous, *Portrait of Jacques Derrida as a Young Jewish Saint*

Gilles Deleuze, *Difference and Repetition*

Gianni Vattimo, *Nihilism and Emancipation: Ethics, Politics, and Law*

Julia Kristeva, *Colette*

Steve Redhead, ed., *The Paul Virilio Reader*

Roland Barthes, *The Neutral: Lecture Course at the Collège de France (1977–1978)*

Gianni Vattimo, *Dialogue with Nietzsche*

Gilles Deleuze, *Nietzsche and Philosophy*

Hélène Cixous, *Dream I Tell You*

Jacques Derrida, *Geneses, Genealogies, Genres, and Genius: The Secrets of the Archive*

Jean Starobinski, *Enchantment: The Seductress in Opera*

Julia Kristeva, *This Incredible Need to Believe*